THE CATHEDRALS OF ENGLAND

1 *Gloucester from the south-east, showing the central tower, 1450–60, the choir clerestory and east window, 1337–50, and the Lady Chapel, c. 1470. Choir probably by William Ramsey; Lady Chapel and tower possibly by John Hobbs*

THE
CATHEDRALS
OF ENGLAND

HARRY BATSFORD

CHARLES FRY

Revised by Bryan Little

LONDON
B. T. BATSFORD LIMITED

First Published, 1934
Tenth Edition, 1960

Revised edition © B. T. Batsford Ltd, 1960

Printed and Bound in Great Britain by Jarrold and Sons Ltd,
London and Norwich for the Publishers

B. T. BATSFORD LTD
4 Fitzhardinge Street, Portman Square, London, W.1

CONTENTS

THE GREATER CATHEDRALS

CONTENTS

THE PARISH-CHURCH CATHEDRALS

MODERN CATHEDRALS

LIST OF ILLUSTRATIONS

ACKNOWLEDGMENT

The publishers wish to thank the following for permission to reproduce the illustrations included in this book:

Hallam Ashley, F.R.P.S. for figs. 35 and 62; Stewart Bale Ltd for fig. 98; *Birmingham Post and Mail* for fig. 94; J. Allan Cash, F.R.P.S. for figs. 16, 49, 82 and 86; the late Brian Clayton for figs. 29, 51, 63, 67, 68, 73 and 93; the late F. H. Crossley for figs. 14, 25 and 27; Eric de Maré for fig. 26; Leo Herbert Felton for figs. 7, 17, 24, 30, 38–40, 45, 58, 70, 71 and 83; F. Frith & Co. for fig. 97; A. F. Kersting for figs. 1, 2, 4–6, 8, 9, 18, 20–23, 28, 31–33, 36, 37, 41, 46–48, 50, 52, 54–57, 61, 64–66, 69, 74, 76–78, 84, 85, 87–92 and 96; W. F. Mansell for fig. 59; National Buildings Record for figs. 17, 44, 80 and 95; J. Dixon Scott for fig. 53; Charles H. Stokes for fig. 13; Edwin Smith for figs. 34 and 43; the late Will Taylor for figs. 3, 11, 42, 60, 72, 75 and 81; Dr Weaver for fig. 10; Reece Winstone, A.R.P.S. for figs. 19 and 79.

2 *Durham: the Norman work in the nave, c. 1099–1128*

3 *Wells: the nave design, late twelfth century*

THE CATHEDRALS AND THEIR BUILDERS

What makes a cathedral is not size, or architectural splendour, or the beauty of its worship, but the possession of a particular piece of church furniture. That necessary object is the *cathedra* (καθέδρα), or ceremonial Throne of the archbishop or bishop who oversees his Christian flock within the area which contains his cathedral town and the building (one might almost say the throne-room) which he has chosen for his working headquarters. The location of the bishop's throne may change from time to time. In some English dioceses this has in fact happened on more than one occasion, and few cathedrals can claim that they stand on a site which has always, since the foundation of a bishopric in their part of England, been that of a cathedral church. Occasionally the bishop of an English diocese has had a *cathedra* in more than one church. But in all cases the essential factor is the presence of that chair, or throne; other aspects of the building are secondary. In practice, England's cathedrals developed, by the end of the Middle Ages, into buildings of large size and great architectural distinction, though we need to remember that they were not, in some dioceses, the largest churches. Thus in men's minds great size and dignity became part of their idea of a cathedral; the disappearance of such abbey churches as those at Glastonbury and Bury St Edmunds increased the architectural lead of those which still contained the bishops' seats. So closely have size and beauty become linked to our conception of a cathedral that parish churches which have come to contain the thrones of newly created bishoprics are often being lengthened and otherwise enlarged. In some districts, Dartmoor for instance or Holderness, the largest and finest parish church is often dubbed the 'cathedral' of the locality concerned. Yet a genuine cathedral could be, and in missionary districts often is, little grander than a tin tabernacle or a timber hut.

The cathedral churches of England which were founded for various purposes in the Middle Ages, and are now used as their cathedrals by the bishops of the Anglican Communion, number thirty-nine; these include Truro which contains alongside its late Victorian fabric an important part of a mediaeval parish church, and Blackburn, which though now a structure entirely later than 1820 is the successor of a mediaeval parish church long used for worship before it. Some of these present-day cathedrals were monastic, collegiate, or parish churches before the Reformation. That at Birmingham was built in the eighteenth century as an additional parish church in a growing industrial town. Those at Liverpool and Guildford are completely new buildings on sites not previously used for worship. There are also in England the sixteen cathedrals of the Roman Catholic church, none as much as 150 years old but all of them fulfilling the essential condition of containing the *cathedra* of an archbishop or bishop.

We shall see that our English cathedrals have a most varied, interesting, and somewhat complex historical background. The Saxon bishops did not, in most cases, place their thrones in the churches with whose cathedral status the later Middle Ages and ourselves have become familiar. The troubled conditions of those early days, with English Christianity in its pioneering days and with frequent attacks from across the sea by pagan invaders, made the bishops of that period apt to move their thrones from one place to another. Some places like Hexham in Northumberland and St Germans in Cornwall were for over a century the cathedrals of pre-Conquest bishops, but were in time deprived of their status. Some Saxon cathedrals, by the middle of the eleventh century, were found in such small, un-important, and undefended places as Elmham in Norfolk, Selsey in Sussex, or Crediton in Devon. Starting with the migration from Crediton to Exeter, and continuing in a series of transfers which formed part of the Norman reorganisation of the Church in England, the seats of some bishops were moved, and in a few cases moved more than once, to more suitably placed towns. Even so, a bishop might still decide to move his headquarters from one part of his diocese to another, so that St John's at Chester and Glastonbury Abbey were both of them cathedrals for a short time but then got 'demoted' from their status. Ely and Carlisle became cathedrals in the twelfth century. The bishop responsible for Somerset had his two cathedrals at Wells and Bath, while the large diocese which included Lancashire and the North-west Midlands had its two episcopal churches at Coventry (a monastic church, not the parish-church cathedral bombed in 1940) and Lichfield.

King Henry VIII made plans to create several new bishoprics; their cathedrals were to be some of the fine churches left empty by the Dissolution of the Monasteries, and their territory was often to correspond more or less closely to counties. The scheme was only partly carried through. But five of our present cathedrals, at Gloucester, Bristol, Oxford, Chester, and

Peterborough, owe their status and their preservation to this stroke of policy. Westminster Abbey was also, though only for the reign of one bishop, a cathedral which obtained this status under Henry VIII.

So things remained till the creation of many more bishoprics in areas grown populous as a result of the Industrial Revolution. The process started with the new dioceses of Ripon and Manchester. It continued for nearly a hundred years. At St Albans, Southwell, and Southwark the thrones of new bishops could be located in churches of obviously cathedralesque type. In most cases, however, large parish churches were taken over, converted, and in some cases enlarged to give more space for diocesan gatherings or for worship of the type one associates with cathedral churches. A scheme to give the Bishop of Manchester a stupendous new Victorian Gothic cathedral was never carried out. The inadequacy of the Anglican and Roman Catholic 'pro-cathedrals' at Liverpool and Guildford, and the bombs which fell on Coventry, have given twentieth-century architects their chance to build cathedrals which are wholly new.

Our study of England's cathedrals is concerned, overwhelmingly, with those built in the Middle Ages. That period can be reckoned as the thousand years which followed the collapse of the Roman Empire. For the first part of it, the spiritual currents of art and thought were feeble and intermittent. But from a phase of disruption and darkness a new building movement was evolved which took form in the so-called Romanesque style which, fostered by Charlemagne and by the rising prestige of the Benedictine Order, began during the ninth century to spread gradually but impressively over Western Europe. Among the conflicting influences that worked on this youthful style the Roman tradition of the basilica, aisled and in its central section barrel vaulted, was long maintained and developed, emerging as a logical and appropriate expression in round-arched forms. Despite a certain laboriousness in construction this style was to hold the field for nearly four centuries with some supreme achievements to its credit, with a characteristic technique of ornament, and a powerful, vigorous school of sculpture. This style was introduced into England some centuries before the Norman Conquest. Many churches were rebuilt in stone. At first its practice must have been crude and provincial enough; yet it is a mistake to regard Anglo-Saxon architecture as other than a simple, more primitive version of the Anglo-Norman which superseded it, and to which it had already been groping its way under influences from across the Channel.

The Saxon cathedrals of England have not left many traces. This is true both of those which were the predecessors of churches still used as cathedrals and of those which at some time or another were deprived of their cathedral status. Excavation has revealed some of the small cathedral at Rochester which stood immediately to the west of the present building, and something has also been discovered of the small apsidal cathedral at Elmham. At Hexham a seventh-century crypt which formed part of St Wilfrid's basilican cathedral survives below the nave of the present priory church; it is built of excellent stone masonry brought from the ruined Roman station of *Corstopitum* (Corbridge) a few miles away. Foundations of this important early Saxon cathedral's eastern apse can also be seen, and above that apse the stone 'Frith Stool' which stands in the later choir was almost certainly the bishop's throne of those early times.

The architectural history of our present cathedrals in the main begins with the Norman Conquest. The building wave which had already clothed Northern France with its 'white robe of churches' swept over England. The majority of its cathedrals have at least a Norman core. Some, like Durham, Norwich, and Peterborough, remain to all intents and purposes Norman fabrics, comparatively little altered at later periods. Others, though elongated, rebuilt, or otherwise transformed, still largely adhere to their Norman planning and proportions. They were planned as cruciform churches, with long naves divided into two by transverse screens; beyond these screens the transepts, the crossings beneath the central towers, and the eastern limbs would contain the choir stalls and also the presbytery where stood the high altar. Numerous chapels projecting from the transepts and eastern aisles would contain small subsidiary altars. The arcades which survive from Norman times in these great churches are massively composed of semi-circular arches, and below the eastern limbs there are sometimes vaulted crypts which were built to contain shrines and additional altars.

Something of the strength and dignity of these Romanesque interiors emerges from photographs of the naves at Durham(*2*), Norwich(*61*), and Peterborough(*66*). But the present severity of these churches belies the smooth perfection of their original covering with a thin coat of plaster which whitened them on the outside, and on the inside formed the basis for elaborately coloured schemes of mural painting. Though built on an unprecedented scale, these churches were on the whole reticent in their carved ornament, the range of this being as a rule limited to a few motifs. The architectural luxury of the Cluniacs was an influence, more widely represented in the churches of that Order and in some parish churches than in the cathedrals (except for Rochester and Ely), which brought a new richness into the work done in the middle decades of the twelfth century.

By about 1150 the Norman Romanesque style had reached its zenith in this country. But its maturity was short-lived, and signs were apparent of an impending break with the Romanesque tradition. Already in the Ile de France and the provinces surrounding it, striking new tendencies were beginning to revolutionise previous architectural conceptions. These, with local experiments in other parts of France, had produced by the middle years of the twelfth century such landmarks in stylistic development as the great churches of St Denis, Sens, Angers, and Pontigny. In England the new tendencies found expression in some interesting experiments which represented a transitional period between Romanesque and Gothic; among the cathedrals this is seen at Worcester and Ripon. The precise currents on which Gothic architecture was borne into this country provide a difficult and controversial problem which is beyond the scope of this book. It is, however, certain that its development cannot be attributed to any single influence, nor must it be forgotten that, while a French master mason was supervising the building of the new choir at Canterbury(23), an English school of the West Country was working out its development of the same idea in the nave at Wells(3). St Hugh's choir at Lincoln (c. 1190) shows both the culmination of the Transitional phase and the inauguration of the building programme of the thirteenth century, and it is significant that the favourite English use of Purbeck marble for shafting and string courses, clumsily employed at Canterbury, here achieved its first maturity.

Northern France had been the forcing house of Gothic architecture, and with the intimate connections between England and the Continent under the Angevin kings it was inevitable that the germ of the new movement should develop rapidly in this country. Yet the evolution of Gothic in England was by no means the same as that in France. At first only tentative experiments followed the whole-hearted metamorphosis which was in progress across the Channel. It was not until the opening years of the thirteenth century that English Gothic established itself as a consistent national architecture, thence developing independently till it finally emerged as a style without any real Continental precedent or parallel.*

* For the chronological nomenclature of this architecture the system evolved by Rickman, while not entirely satisfactory, seems to be the most practical for ordinary purposes. Its six divisions are mainly based on the styles of window tracery as follows: Norman, Transitional, Early English, Geometrical, Decorated, and Perpendicular.

In the thirteenth century the English builders consolidated their national idiom; this was particularly distinguished from most Continental examples by its preference for the square east end as against that which had a round or polygonal apse. The great churches of England were also, for the most part, much lower in proportion to their other dimensions than their counterparts in France. The Early English style, if not to be compared in grandeur or daring to that current in Northern France, at least had its distinctive grace, finely represented in the cathedrals of Salisbury, Lincoln, and Wells. Here were churches conceived on a new scale of splendour, but independent of monastic influence and mainly built as the seats of bishops, expressing something of the princeliness of the prelate-statesmen concerned in their building. Their planning marked a definite departure from tradition, involving a transformation of the eastern limb, with a lengthening of the presbytery to give more accommodation for the canons. Beyond the high altar, a processional path led to an eastward extension, or retrochoir, built to house the shrine of the local saint. Small eastern transepts were often built to provide additional altars for the canons' daily Masses, and, with the rising English cult of Our Lady, a Lady Chapel was often added at the extreme east end. Certain features, however, were generally borrowed from the plan of monastic buildings; among these were the cloisters, generally used in the secular cathedrals for Sunday processions, and the chapter-house which was usually built as a well-lit polygon, loftily vaulted from a central pier.

Professor Prior well characterised this thirteenth-century English style as 'an art of slender shaftings of Purbeck marble, pointed lancets, wall arcades ranged one behind the other, level-crowned vaults, with multiplied string courses of marble, arch-moulds of many members, some adorned with the dog-tooth, and often with a free and varied carving of white stone in label-heads and capitals—and finally it had a splendid free figure sculpture. So we have it at St Hugh's Cathedral at Lincoln and in the Ely Galilee, then at Salisbury, and in all the great works of the thirteenth century in England.' Though generally effective in the design of its façades this period seldom rose to striking heights save in the great sculptured screens of its west fronts. Two fine examples are the dissimilar triumphs of Peterborough (65) and Wells (82), the latter being conceived as little more than a background for the display of some of the finest figure carving in England—a plastic revelation by west-country craftsmen of the didactic aims of mediaeval religious art. The style reached its summit after the middle of the century,

4 *Lincoln: the Angel Choir, 1256–80, probably designed by Simon of Thirsk*

5   Ely: arcading in the Lady Chapel, c. 1330

7   Chichester: Romanesque relief, probably c. 1130–40

8 (top)   Lincoln: late f
9 (bottom)   Salisbury: spandrel

6 *Worcester: late Perpendicular chantry of Prince Arthur*

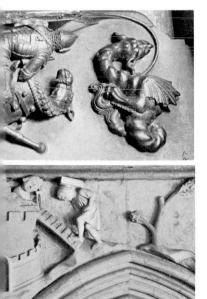

...entury misericord in St Hugh's choir
...b-century wall-arcade in the chapter-house

10 *Ely: entrance to chantry of Bishop Alcock (d. 1500)*

11 *Exeter: the nave, c. 1328–42, showing minstrels' gallery; mostly designed by Thomas Witney. The marble font is of 1684*

when the lancets and plate tracery of its fenestration were superseded by larger windows whose heads were patterned with the precise, wiry stone designs which characterise the Geometrical phase. Lincoln Cathedral is perhaps the best barometer of thirteenth-century change, and its eastward culmination in the famous Angel Choir (finished 1280) not only displays the full maturity of this art in England but foreshadows the rich development of the next century (4).

'Geometrical' does in fact mark the transition from the formal seriousness of thirteenth-century art to the romantic, luxuriant style of the fourteenth century. This latter was influenced by the picturesque brilliance of the English Age of Chivalry. Its predominant constructional discovery was the sinuous ogee arch, enhanced by crocketing and applied as a favourite motif in rich surface treatment. While Geometrical elements were sometimes retained in window tracery, there was in general a relaxation into free-flowing or curvilinear forms which constitutes one of the most attractive and individual developments of English Gothic. Such gaily imaginative achievements as the east window at Carlisle (24) and the west window at York (92) are without any exact Continental parallel; their colour seems quickened as with the flickering of wings. Accomplished local schools emerged in East Anglia where the curvilinear fashion persisted into the next century, and in the North where the west front of York Minster was built with a luxury unprecedented even in its own period. Yet generally speaking this manner is somewhat sparsely represented among our cathedrals, though the naturalistic revolution in carving found expression in the spring-time exuberance of such smaller works as the chapter-house at Southwell. But its crowning achievement is at Exeter, where a famous line of building bishops left a triumphant monument to the skill and fecundity of local craftsmanship in an interior (11) which, in its sensuous warmth of moulded marble and luxuriance of freestone carving, brings a worldly, almost pagan note into Gothic architecture.

The catastrophe of the Black Death may have almost extinguished this rich school. But already the Court masons, along with those in the lower Severn valley and elsewhere, had been sowing the seeds of an architectural revolution. This found some of its first fruits in St Stephen's Chapel at Westminster, and (from about 1340) in the recasing of the Norman presbytery at Gloucester with a rectilinear cage of light masonry (44); this unified its interior into a lofty design crowned by a clerestory of tall windows which appeared to be a single structure of stone and glass. The results of these building operations were far-reaching, for they inaugurated a system of economical yet almost consistently effective surface treatment which was to endure in England longer than all the previous Gothic styles combined. This new Perpendicular manner found immediate adoption; well before the end of the fourteenth century it was used with notable effect in the naves at Winchester(87) and Canterbury(22). In 1540 it was still flourishing, and even as late as 1640 was occasionally employed in such strongholds of conservatism as the Universities. Though the achievement of Gloucester's choir was never quite surpassed, the maturity of the style is delightfully expressed in the Lady Chapel(45) of the same cathedral (c. 1470) which typifies in miniature the English churches and chapels of the fifteenth century—lofty, rectangular, aisleless halls, built as it were of glass set in panelling, and roofed either with lierne vaults or with the lovely development of fan vaulting. This fan vaulting is first seen in the cloisters at Gloucester(42) and reached its climax in the retrochoir at Peterborough(64) and in the magnificent chapels of St George's Windsor, King's College at Cambridge, and Henry VII's at Westminster. But the aspect of Perpendicular which left its most conspicuous mark on the cathedrals was the tower-building which produced, as the last splendours of the live Gothic tradition, the grand, exuberant piles which raise their heads over the central spaces at Worcester and Gloucester, York and Canterbury, with their burden of deep-toned bells which were already, by the end of the fifteenth century, tolling the decline of mediaeval ways of life, art, and thought.

We have now briefly to consider the men responsible for the building of these churches. As the subject includes the whole problem of the identity and work of the mediaeval architect, and the complex organisation of the mediaeval building trade, it can only shortly be treated here.

In the eleventh and twelfth centuries the clergy employed many unskilled labourers to supplement the small supply of skilled professional masons; to this fact, perhaps, is due the somewhat rough and ready nature of some Romanesque stonework, and the structural collapse which occurred in some English cathedrals built at that time. By about 1150 the building trade seems to have achieved a measure of independence, and to have organised its own 'lodges'. These 'lodges', composed of travelling masons rather than of the more static urban craftsmen banded together in guilds, were the organisations to which the masons of the Middle Ages belonged; as comparatively few mediaeval buildings were built of squared and dressed masonry, they would be more apt than carpenters and unskilled workmen to travel to the places where work was in hand. They were directed by a small number of really skilled master masons, and it is to these men that the credit for the evolution of mediaeval architecture undoubtedly belongs. The researches of Mr L. F. Salzmann and Mr John Harvey have thrown a flood of light on all these activities, particularly in the later mediaeval period from which more documents have survived. The famous sacrists, priors, and bishops who have been credited with individual architectural achievements can seldom have been responsible for more than the orders, and for some of the business organisation which was needed for the work's success. At first the materials were mainly worked or finished on the spot. But the Purbeck marble which was popular as a thirteenth-century decorative element was an exception, being dressed and worked in the Dorset quarries. As time went on the practice of specialised 'shopwork' in local centres became increasingly common, as with the alabaster tombs from Derbyshire and the Norfolk fonts. By the end of the fourteenth century it may be assumed that most carving and decorative work beyond the ordinary run was delivered in sections from the craft workshops of the leading cities.

The workmen were latterly of three grades. First came the *cementarii* or *lathotomi*—the cutting masons who carried out the more ambitious work of moulding and carving in good quality stone. Secondly came the layers, setters, or wallers. Last of all were the rough layers and hard hewers—the men who dressed the large stone blocks and were responsible for the rougher and plainer types of masonry. In addition, there were the 'imagers', or carvers of statues and other figures. To the freemasons and imagers, along with the highly important carpenters and glaziers, we owe the superb works of art and craftsmanship of which our cathedrals, despite many vicissitudes, are still the repositories. The fertile art of the stone carver appears in the working of capitals, corbels, arcading, bosses, pinnacled tabernacle work and niches, and in the splendid funeral craft of tombs, monuments, and chantries. The schemes of coloured decoration have mostly vanished, and of the glories of the stained glass which largely survived the Reformation, much was smashed later by Puritan zeal. Yet what remains at York, Canterbury, Lincoln, and elsewhere testifies to the excellence of the craft. Towards the close of the fourteenth century, carpentry reached its zenith in this country, communicating something of its rich delicacy to the stone-carver's technique. The stallwork at Lincoln, Chester(27), and Manchester marks the florescence of this craft, but the tradition endured beyond the Reformation, and we see it recur in Bishop Cosin's lovely font cover(32) and stalls at Durham, and later in the carving done by Grinling Gibbons and his colleagues in St Paul's.

The working régime of the English cathedrals in the actual period of the Middle Ages is apt to be a little confusing, particularly to students from abroad. In nine of them (York, St Paul's, Lincoln, Wells, Lichfield, Chichester, Salisbury, Hereford, and Exeter) the services were conducted by secular canons; they eventually came under the rule of a Dean who had such subordinate officers to assist him as the Chancellor, Treasurer, and Precentor. The houses of these officials lay within the Close and were grouped around that area in no particular order. As members of the chapter were often, for various reasons, away from their cathedrals their places in choir would be taken by the junior clergy known as vicars choral, and the 'Colleges' of these vicars are still particularly attractive features of the precincts at Wells and Hereford.

The cathedrals at Canterbury, Rochester, Winchester, Bath, Worcester, Coventry, Ely, Norwich, and Durham were also the churches of important Benedictine monasteries, the nominal abbot being the bishop of the diocese and the actual head of the community being styled the prior. As in other monasteries the buildings, of which the refectory, dormitory, and chapter-house were the most important, were compactly arranged around a cloister, and these arrangements can still be seen particularly well at Durham, as well as at Chester and Gloucester which were Benedictine abbeys before they became cathedrals under Henry VIII. Carlisle Cathedral was served by Augustinian regular canons whose life was on the monastic pattern and whose buildings were similar to those of a Benedictine abbey. We have also seen how Henry VIII turned six monastic churches (including Westminster Abbey) into cathedrals, and how numerous buildings, of varying past status, have become the cathedrals of modern bishoprics.

Such historic points lead us naturally to the nature of the worship that was carried on in the mediaeval cathedrals, and to the relationship of those great buildings with the parish churches where the laity normally went to church. Both in monastic and secular cathedrals the main function of the clergy was the regular performance, in as splendid and dignified a manner as was possible, of the *Opus Dei*, or ceremonial worship of the Church. The main elements in this were the conventual or capitular High Mass, and the chanting in choir of such Offices as Prime, Terce, Vespers, and Compline. The choir services, in particular, were something not to be found on such a scale in the ordinary parish churches. Their worthy rendering, by liturgical and musical experts who were gathered together first and foremost for this purpose, and who took their due places in the properly furnished choirs of the churches, was the main purpose for which these monastic and collegiate buildings (whether or not they happened to be cathedrals) were built, extended, and adorned. Very few of the laity would ever attend these services, and their presence or absence was irrelevant to its completeness; the parish churches were the normal scene of their devotions. In some churches of monks or canons regular a portion of the nave continued to be used by parishioners, but, if so, this section of it was clearly partitioned from the choir by solid screens so that in effect the building contained not one place of worship but two. The only reason for which large numbers of the laity would be admitted to the eastern part of a great monastic or collegiate church would be to visit the shrines of saints, and to venerate the relics contained therein. But those shrines themselves would also be in a clearly defined part of the church, and these pilgrims' visits would not involve any entrance to the choir with its high altar and stalls. The choirs of the greatest monastic churches would be of much the same size, whether or not they happened to contain a bishop's throne. Among the 'college' churches of secular canons those enjoying cathedral status would as a rule be larger than those like Ottery St Mary or St Mary's at Warwick which did not have that rank. Yet Beverley, Ripon, Southwell, and St George's at Windsor prove that such secular colleges could sometimes have churches as large as the smaller cathedrals such as Rochester or Carlisle.

Such considerations bring one on to the numerous adaptations, re-furnishings, and restorations which our cathedrals have witnessed in the last four centuries. Under Henry VIII the system of a secular Dean and Chapter was extended to those whose clergy had previously been monks or canons regular.* In a few more years the services changed from the Latin Mass and the numerous choir Offices to the English services of the Prayer Book. In this process the choir services (of mattins and evensong) became more dominant than before, and with the disappearance of shrines and side altars the choir, with one altar, became the one centre of regular activity. But there was no question of destroying that intimacy of worship which had been so great a feature of the rigidly subdivided pre-Reformation cathedrals. It was rightly seen that neither liturgically nor aesthetically does it make sense to open out into a single compartment a long, comparatively narrow

* Hence the name 'College Green' for part of the precincts at Gloucester and Bristol.

building meant to be divided at least into two main sections. So in the seventeenth and eighteenth centuries, as one may see from many old prints and engravings, screens were always retained, and those screens were topped by the large organs, in their splendidly carved cases, which were now available; such cathedrals as Gloucester and Exeter continue this division which made for a properly enclosed choir, while leaving the nave for special occasions. In our own time, if altar services are desired in the nave, then a nave altar should be, and sometimes is, installed. But for a congregation in the nave a high altar up in the choir, even if the removal of the solid screen has made it visible from the cathedral's west end, is much too distant for close participation in the worship of a sanctuary which may be as much as three hundred feet away.*

Apart from continuing this division of our cathedrals, the Stuart and Georgian period, particularly after the Restoration in 1660, saw great activity in the refurnishing of the choirs which were the part of the buildings most constantly in use. Stalls and altarpieces were often put in, some of them of real artistic merit and dignity, though not always in any of the Gothic styles. In the later years of the eighteenth century and fairly soon after 1800 a good many fittings in what may be called 'churchwarden' Gothic were inserted. These Stuart and Georgian fittings were considered incongruous and tasteless by the Victorians, and most of them were cast out in favour of greatly inferior fittings in their particular Gothic taste. Some Renaissance organ cases, however, survive, and at Canterbury we can still see some splendid stallwork in the Wren manner. More important still, in many cathedrals a feature adding greatly to their artistic interest, and better appreciated now than ever before, are the post-Reformation tombs and mural monuments in the various styles from Elizabethan Renaissance to Greek Revival. Baroque side altars, such as one finds in Catholic churches abroad, were naturally lacking in the Protestant England of those times, but here, to some extent, we find our sculptural compensation.

The passion for 'vistas', and for the unitary treatment of interior spaces, in the meantime gained much ground and was responsible for ruining many a cathedral interior. This tendency started in the eighteenth century, when some cathedrals like Lichfield had their choirs and Lady Chapels opened out into single compartments so that the one altar in such a building stood

---

* See also Bishop John Milner's dictum, in his Winchester history of 1798, that it is 'a preposterous attempt, against the nature and plan of a Gothic cathedral . . . to aim at reducing it to one great chamber'.

far away against the extreme east wall. The Victorians, under the influence of the Oxford Movement, replaced high altars on or near their original sites, but in several cathedrals they also opened out disastrous vistas in the other direction by demolishing mediaeval or later screens. In some cathedrals they then inadequately partitioned naves from choirs by spindly, metallic devilments in the worst possible taste and construction. In fairness to them, however, we must remember that similar tactics were at the same time being followed in many Gothic cathedrals on the Continent, the mistaken idea being held that a mediaeval cathedral with a long choir can be handled inside like the 'openly planned' Gesú at Rome, whose sanctuary projects only a short way beyond the space beneath its dome. At the same time, the Victorians, especially Sir Gilbert Scott, did much structural work. In many cathedrals heavy repairs were made absolutely necessary by the condition of the buildings. In others the restoration was much less easy to justify from the historic point of view, for various work of the later Middle Ages was swept away to make buildings look as the Victorians imagined they had looked when new. Perpendicular windows, being in a style which was then thought debased, suffered particularly in this slaughter of the traces of historic evolution.

Our consideration of the work done by the Victorians in our ancient cathedrals leads on to a brief passage on a group of cathedral churches which are almost all Victorian. These are the cathedrals of the Roman Catholics. As none of them are old, and as not all possess architectural merit or impressiveness, they are apt to be disregarded by visitors who are not Roman Catholics. Yet all are cathedrals in the full sense of the word, while some, on any reckoning, are worth seeing as specimens of modern church architecture. In one, at Westminster, the *Opus Dei* is daily rendered, in a manner in general akin to that which prevailed in the Middle Ages, with a dignity and splendour which command the greatest admiration; allow for such factors as birettas, Byzantine arches, and the lack of a screen, and Westminster is inevitably nearer than the Anglican cathedrals can be to what was done in England's cathedrals before the Reformation.

Some of the Roman Catholic cathedrals, like the one at Newcastle, designed by Pugin in a pleasant version of the Decorated style and built (except for its fine spire) in the 1840s, were erected as parish churches before the Roman Catholic hierarchy was re-established in this country. Others were specially built as cathedrals. Brompton Oratory, having for some years contained the throne of the Archbishop of Westminster, can claim the status of an 'ex-cathedral'. At Northampton new transepts, a tower, and a chancel have recently been added to make the building correspond more closely, like some of the Church of England's parish-church cathedrals, to modern ideas of what a cathedral should be like.

Of the others, one may briefly mention a few without giving them complete treatment in a special section of this book. At Clifton the 'procathedral' of the Apostles is in its main structure the oldest of them all, for it was started in 1834, and had it been completed according to the architect Goodridge's original plans it would have been among the most important Greek Revival churches in the country. Pugin's work appears at Nottingham, and more notably at Birmingham where his interior, within a building whose brick exterior is somewhat forbidding in a gauntly Flemish manner, shows both Pugin himself and Hardman his glazier to splendid advantage. More important still is Pugin's Roman Catholic cathedral at Southwark, designed as St George's parish church, soon raised to cathedral status, and restored since its bombing (with a clerestory for which there was no money in Pugin's time) more nearly in accordance with its architect's designs. The east window is of special beauty and the whole interior, with a more Perpendicular feeling than it had before the bombing, is most dignified and effective; it is something which visitors to London should not miss. At Salford the cruciform building, by Hadfield and Weightmann and built about 1845, is of considerable dignity with its vaulted choir in the Decorated manner; this cathedral is also an astonishing pot-pourri of borrowings from mediaeval Gothic in the North of England. At Plymouth the Roman Catholic cathedral has had less attention than its architectural merits deserve; its needle-slender spire is of astonishing grace and is the tallest feature of the city's skyline.

Coming nearer to our own time, Bentley's great basilican cathedral at Westminster is among the noblest places of Christian worship put up in this country within the last hundred years. In its general design it is adapted from the basilica of Maxentius at Rome, but it is more fully Byzantine in the interior decoration of marble and mosaics which has so far been carried out. Its slender *campanile* is a well-known part of London's skyline. By contrast, the far smaller cathedral at Leeds is a charming work built between 1902 and 1904; its Gothic by J. H. Eastwood is recognisably post-Victorian and is what one associates with the Arts and Crafts movement and the work of such designers as Leonard Stokes or Sir Giles Gilbert Scott in his great Anglican cathedral at Liverpool(*12*). In Liverpool, moreover, the architectural story of the Roman Catholic cathedral is already of the

12 *Liverpool: the eastern crossing and choir stalls of the new cathedral, designed by Sir Giles Gilbert Scott*

13 Exeter: the late Perpendicular tombs of Bishops
14 (above, right) Southwell: the alabaster tomb
15 (below, left) Canterbury: the tomb of the Black
16 Winchester: the tomb of William of Wykeham
17 (below, right) Winchester: Cheere's monumen

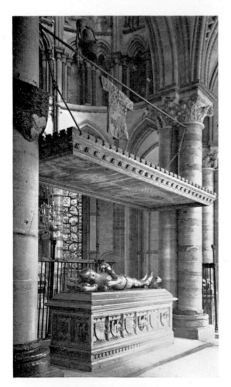

(d. 1280) and Stafford (d. 1419)
...op Sandys (d. 1588)
...l. 1376)

...Willis (d. 1734)

18 *Bristol from the south-east, showing the twelfth-century choir and the central tower, c. 1466–71*

19 *Bristol: the openwork vaulting of the south choir aisle*

20 *Bristol: the choir, c. 1330, looking east*

greatest interest. For Lutyens, in the early 1930s, produced designs for a vast domed cathedral, in a modernised version of the Renaissance or Mannerist style, whose size would almost have equalled that of St Peter's in Rome. The crypt of this cathedral has actually been built, and one can see exterior masonry of a grandeur very typical of its designer. Inside, the dark brickwork, the cross arches, and tunnel vaults are all impressive, and the burial chapel of Archbishops Whiteside and Downey is a work of great beauty. The whole structure is a work by a great architect—a fragment, yet enough to make one realise how fine a building we have missed. The main design had to be abandoned for financial reasons; so too (most fortunately) has a reduced version of it which would also have had a dome. The whole matter is now being considered again, and a competition is being held to obtain designs for a new cathedral within a price limit of about £1,000,000. The chief architectural assessor is Mr Basil Spence; one may hope that what is built will be as challenging a building as that which Mr Spence himself is now completing for the Anglicans at Coventry.

Such thoughts bring us back to the way in which Anglican cathedrals are faring in our own century. So far as their main structure is concerned, the 'major' cathedrals have not received many additions, though exceptions occur in the nave at Southwark and in the eastern-most chapel at Norwich. Much excellent work has, however, been done to ensure their basic stability, and vast sums have recently been laid out, or are being spent, on cleaning and renewing decayed external stonework. Inside, the most evident feature has been the continued and loving care which chapters have given to fabrics and furnishings. Work has been done in choirs, naves, Lady Chapels, and side chapels. Tombs and mural monuments have often been beautifully cleaned and recoloured.

Architecturally speaking, the most important developments are those seen in some parish-church cathedrals, reflecting the modern Englishman's sense of what he feels essential to a cathedral's nature. In his view a cathedral must be large, with transepts, a central tower, a Lady Chapel, and some other chapels. It must, in other words, be as unlike as possible to nearly all ancient (and most modern) parish churches. Large additions are thus being made to some parish-church cathedrals, in some cases converting rectangular churches into cruciform buildings. In no case can one yet pass a final artistic judgment on these activities. One must, however, remember that the cathedral status of these churches will not be altered provided they retain their bishops' *cathedrae*.

THE GREATER CATHEDRALS

BRISTOL

The Cathedral Church of the Holy and Undivided Trinity

The Augustinian abbey of St Augustine was founded about 1140 by Robert Fitzharding, who later obtained from Henry II the grant of the forfeited Berkeley estates. The connection of his family with this abbey continued all through the Middle Ages, as may still be seen from the series of Berkeley monuments, and from the figures and heraldry of the fourteenth-century glass. Though only the choir, transepts, and central tower of the mediaeval building survive, and though these have undergone considerable alteration, much of the design of this cathedral (whose episcopal status came in 1542) is so unusual and original that the building is of the highest interest and architectural importance. Of the original late Norman church only some masonry in the south transept remains visible. In the thirteenth century the original (now 'Elder') Lady Chapel was added east of the north transept. The greatest period of reconstruction was the early fourteenth century under Abbot Knowle (1306–1332). This saw the building of the present eastern limb, with its little sacristy on the south side and also, in all probability, the 'Berkeley' Chapel which leads out of it. Under Abbot Snow (1332–1341) the Newton chapel, with the treasury above it, was added off the south transept. The transept vaults and central tower were put up late in the fifteenth century, being probably finished under Abbot Newland, or Nailheart (1481–1515).

A chronicle of Newland's time preserved at Berkeley Castle is an important source for this Bristol abbey's history. By the time of the Dissolution in 1539 a start had been made with the building of a new nave, but nothing more was done on this after the establishment of the see, and the cathedral, truncated and on a small scale, remained without a nave till 1868 when work on a new nave was begun to Street's design. The beautiful sixteenth-century screen was arbitrarily removed by Dean Elliott in 1860, but portions of it have now been re-erected as a parclose. Pearson's work of the 1890s included the restoration of the Elder Lady Chapel, the repair of the central

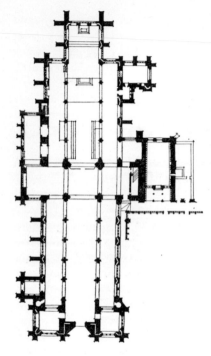

tower, and the erection, on an unduly lofty scale, of the present reredos on the site of the mediaeval one. The choir screen was also made to his designs.

Except for the towers, the main features of the design can most advantageously be grasped from within. Street's nave and western towers blend well with the fourteenth-century eastern limb, the nave's design being closely adapted from that of Knowle's choir. The western towers, however, and the west front, with their obviously French Gothic influences, form a somewhat pedantic composition. Crowned by its burly central tower, the cathedral is best seen from the lower ground to the south (18); the absence of a triforium and clerestory is very marked, but the tall transomed windows of the choir and Lady Chapel make a fine range. Inside, the Early English Elder Lady Chapel, with its Geometrical east window, is a pleasant early Gothic work; it has characteristic wall arcading with fine spandrel carving that was probably done by sculptors who also worked on the west front at Wells. But it is in the design of the choir that the bold originality of the fourteenth-century Bristol masons is most apparent. This 'hall-church' design is unique among English cathedrals in that the aisles are as high as the central section, though there are many unvaulted churches of similar design in the South-West and somewhat similar 'spatial' arrangements occur in Anjou and in Germany, and in the choir of the Temple Church in London. Here at Bristol, while the main vault (20), with its ingeniously cusped ribs, is of normal design, the aisle vaults (19) are both complex and unique. From each pier, and performing the function of an interior flying buttress, a solid stone transom is thrown across the aisle to connect with the massive external buttresses. Each transom is sustained by a transverse pointed arch, with pierced patterns in the spandrels and delightful little carvings along the actual transoms. From the centre of each transom there springs an inverted pyramid of masonry which rises to ridge ribs on either side, thus forming a series of separate compartments of transverse tunnel vaulting, each one of which corresponds to one of the tall arches of the main arcade. This arrangement, perhaps more notable for its originality and ingenuity than for its beauty, forms an interesting experiment in a novel technique of skeleton masonry that was soon to reach its culmination, perhaps by the same school of crafts-men, in the remodelling of the choir at Gloucester. The unaisled Lady Chapel, with its splendid fourteenth-century reredos, is of more conventional design, though in its unusual upper passageway (in default of a triforium gallery) it continues some elements from the aisled portion of the eastern limb. The great east window is of a striking curvilinear design, with some fine original heraldic glass in the traceries.

The openwork vault of the sacristy, with its 'flying' ribs, was another original contribution by these Bristol designers, being quickly imitated at St David's, as was the 'stellar' work which is a rare feature of the unusually designed series of similar tomb recesses provided in the choir aisles and Lady Chapel. Of the actual memorials within these recesses the most splendid, with its fine mitred effigy and canopied work along the front, is that of Abbot Newbury who died in 1473; Abbots Hunt (d. 1481) and Newland have similar stone effigies, while chain-mailed Berkeley figures and Baily's fine bust of the Bristol-born writer Robert Southey occupy some of the others. The post-Reformation monuments in Bristol Cathedral are of much variety and interest. Sir Charles Vaughan's is a good piece of seventeenth-century Renaissance work in the manner of Nicholas Stone, and the Greek Revival is represented by a good group of murals by Chantrey, Baily, and others. The Georgian murals are numerous and include a fine composition by James Paine to William Powell the actor. Others com-memorate people who died when unsuccessfully seeking health at the Bristol resorts of Hotwells and Clifton; they include a beautiful one by the younger Bacon to Mrs Elizabeth Draper (Lawrence Sterne's 'Eliza') who died in 1778.

The late Norman chapter-house was built soon after 1155, the eastern bay being demolished soon after damage in the famous Bristol Riots of 1831. It is richly vaulted and arcaded, and with its beautiful pillared and vaulted vestibule is the finest Norman chapter-house in the country. The lower part of the much-restored gateway to College Green is of a similar design, but its upper part was rebuilt about 1515 and nowadays is largely modern. Other remains of the monastic buildings, though comparatively slight, are incorporated in the Cathedral School. The picturesque night stairs, however, survive and lead down into the south transept.

CANTERBURY
The Cathedral of Christ Church

The late Saxon basilican church, of considerable size and architectural pretension and with its relics of various early saints, was destroyed soon after the Norman Conquest. Work on a new cathedral and its attendant Benedictine monastery was begun in 1070 under Lanfranc, the first archbishop of the Norman period. It was an unambitious scheme, hurriedly completed in seven years and based on the Conqueror's abbey church at Caen whence Lanfranc had come to rule at Canterbury. This church soon became inadequate for the seat of the primate and a choir of over a hundred monks, so by direction of St Anselm (1093–1114) the eastern limb was enlarged under Priors Ernulph and Conrad; much of their work is still visible in the crypt and from outside. The glory of 'Conrad's Choir' was short-lived, for in 1174 it was gutted by fire. It was significant for the course of early Gothic in England that from among the *artifices* assembled to do the repairs a Frenchman, William of Sens who must already have been concerned with the building of Sens Cathedral, was chosen as master mason. The precise degree of French influence in the design of Canterbury's reconstructed choir has been the cause of much controversy. Four years after the start of the work the French master mason was crippled by a fall from the scaffolding, his place being taken by one William 'the Englishman' who completed the new eastern limb in 1184. Though the most cursory glance at the rising style of the Ile de France discloses the French elements in the Canterbury design—the great projection of the buttresses, the characteristic lancets, coupled columns, arch-moulds, and 'Corinthian' capitals—there is at the same time much that is indigenous and prophetic of the English vernacular of the next century: notably the lavish use of dark Purbeck marble for detached carving and string courses, and a rising school of freestone carving. When one remembers that the monks had stipulated that their choir was to be rebuilt within the shell of the older church, the task of analysis becomes still more complex. The final assumption must be that the work represents a compromise, not un-characteristic of English cathedral art, between the wishes of the patrons, the natural inclinations of a French designer, and the instincts of native crafts-men working out the matter for themselves.

Four years before the fire of 1174 the most significant event in the mediaeval history of the cathedral occurred. This was the murder of Becket in 1170. The martyr's fame spread rapidly through-out Europe, and his shrine at Canterbury became one of the most popular places of pilgrimage in the Middle Ages. In 1220 the relics were solemnly transferred from the crypt to the Trinity Chapel, east of the high altar. For the next three centuries

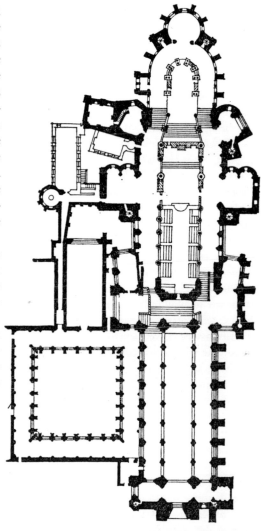

countless pilgrims, including kings, princes, and cardinals, with crowds of the poor and diseased and those prosperous 'middling' people so neatly drawn by Chaucer, journeyed to the shrine with offerings ranging from Louis VII of France's carbuncle jewel the size of an egg to the halfpence in the palm of a beggar. Early in the sixteenth century, when the offerings had considerably fallen, the shrine's annual income was over £4,000 (a vast sum for that period and equivalent to at least £120,000 now). Erasmus, visiting the shrine, remarked how 'the meanest part was gold, every part glistened, shone, and sparkled with very large jewels, some of them exceeding the size of a goose's egg'. Late in the fourteenth century the monks at last decided to replace Lanfranc's archaic nave and transepts; the present work, which would have been in progress when Chaucer's pilgrims visited the cathedral, was carried out under Prior Chillenden between 1379 and 1405. St Michael's Chapel and the Lady Chapel were added in the fifteenth century, while between about 1490 and 1503 John Wastell raised the lovely central tower to replace the Norman 'Angel Steeple'. In 1538 Henry VIII issued his famous writ against Becket for 'treason, contumacy, and rebellion' which was read before the saint's shrine. The suit was tried at Westminster, and in the absence of a defendant had its inevitable sequel in the removal of the gold and jewels of Canterbury in 26 cartloads to the royal treasury. Such treasures as escaped the Reformation, particularly windows, were many of them destroyed by the Puritans under Richard Culmer (notorious as 'Blue Dick'), though a considerable portion of the magnificent early glass remained miraculously undamaged. Since the Reformation the fabric has been carefully tended, and except for the unfortunate removal, in 1834, of the north-west tower which still remained from Lanfranc's cathedral, it has on the whole suffered little from modern restorers.

The cathedral lies in a saucer of green hills, and some of the loveliest views of it are to be had from the crests of the roads leading into the city, as at Harbledown, where Chaucer's party made its last halt, and where pilgrims would fall on their knees at the first sight of the golden angel above the central tower. 'Tanta majestate sese erigit in coelum', wrote Erasmus, recording an impression with an unaccustomed note of emotion, 'ut procul etiam intuentibus religionem incutiat'. Today the angel has vanished and the city has spread its bounds about the cathedral which rises pale and shapely above the rooftops, its three towers grouping unforgettably against their background of Kentish fields and woods. Nearer at hand, a superb view of the cathedral was opened up by the heavy bomb damage, in High Street and Burgate Street, caused by the 'Baedeker' raids, and this view has been well retained and exploited in the excellent contemporary development of that area. From other directions roads approach the cathedral through mediaeval gateways, and a network of narrow, busy streets, overhanging houses, and rather forlorn little parish churches surrounds the broad *enceinte*

21 Canterbury from the south-west. Nave designed by Henry Yevele, 1378-1405; south-west tower by Thomas Mapilton, 1423-34; central tower by John Wastell, 1490-97; north-west tower by Blore, 1834-35

22 Canterbury: the nave, showing the Carolean font. Arcades and vault by Henry Yevele, 1391–1405, strainer arch by John Wastell, c. 1490

23 Canterbury: the choir, designed by William of Sens, 1175–78

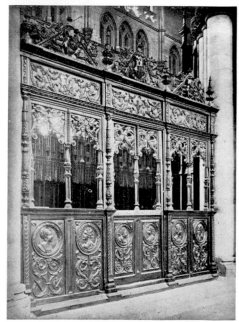

25 Carlisle: the Renaissance screen of Prior
(later Dean) Salkeld, c. 1542

of what once ranked among the greatest and richest of European monasteries. Considerable remains of the cathedral priory exist substantially intact, in ruins, or worked into later buildings; many of these are now used by the King's School. The Close at Canterbury is, indeed, one of the most fascinating architectural mazes in England.

The cathedral's west front, of *c*. 1400–1458 (except for the north-west tower which was built, in the 1830s, as a copy of the 'Chichele' tower), is an effective, well-proportioned composition, though later houses prevent its being seen to the best advantage; the shallow western porch has good lierne vaulting and bosses recalling those in a similar position at Winchester. Henry Yevele's nave (21) forms a fine, lofty range, early Perpendicular in style but with Decorated elements in some of the tracery design. In the south aisle are the tallest aisle windows in England, but those on the north side are shortened to allow for the cloisters which abut against this side of the church. The Perpendicular architecture of the nave is continued in the western transepts where the great windows are of striking beauty, that on the south being flanked by a single large pinnacle. Rising to 235 feet the central tower ('Bell Harry') is unsurpassed of its type, a splendid, exuberant achievement in the cheerful English craft of tower building which seems to refute, at its close, the pessimism of the fifteenth century. Beyond the western transepts there begins the earlier, complex sequence of the choir and its eastward extension. At first, the outer walls of this eastern limb (including the delightful pair of slim arcaded towers against the eastern transepts, the interlaced wall arcading, the apses of the transeptal chapels,* and the larger chapels which project some way towards the Trinity Chapel) belong largely to the Norman choir of Prior Conrad. However, the graceful lancets arranged in couples round William the Englishman's apse, and the tall, thin buttresses show the stage when the influence of early French Gothic had come in. The inward contraction of the east end was due to the retention of the unburnt Norman Chapels of St Andrew and St Anselm which still lead out of the presbytery aisles; the latter chapel has a large, interesting Decorated window of the Kentish type which in all cost £42 17s. 2d., when inserted in 1336. The building ends in the remarkable Corona, or 'Becket's Crown', which remains an architectural puzzle. As it lacks its final storeys it has never been discovered how it was intended to complete this rather gaunt curving tower of Gallic lancets and

* They almost certainly inspired those projecting from the transepts of St Hugh's choir at Lincoln.

emaciated buttresses which stands unfinished and ending, so to speak, in the air.

As one enters the cathedral at the west end the early Perpendicular nave (22) of nine bays, though short for England, is a work of consummate grace and refinement, built with an economy of stonework which lends a feeling of space to its moderate length and width. The obvious comparison is with the nave at Winchester which is practically its contemporary. But at the latter the bosses are far larger and finer than at Canterbury, and the surviving Norman core of the pillars caused close spacing and solid construction. At Canterbury, however, the builders of a wholly new nave were free to indulge a whim for constructional lightness which is carried rather to excess. The elongation of the piers at the expense of the upper storeys can certainly be criticised, and the design is really of two storeys, as the triforium is only the downward extension of the clerestory windows whose disproportionate smallness recalls the small clerestory of the slightly later nave at Seville Cathedral. The main lighting has thus to come from the large aisle windows. The arches of the arcades, and the light, lofty vaults spring from shafts grouped against the moulded piers, each one with its neat and separate capital. Except in the west window little old glass remains, and there are no old fittings except for the lovely painted marble Carolean font of 1639 and fine classical canopy of the Restoration archbishop's throne which has been put at the entrance of St Augustine's Chapel below the north-western tower.

The crossing affords the most beautiful views in the cathedral; the strainer arches, or stone girders, across two of the tower arches and some other arches in the nave and aisles, were built early in the sixteenth century to help support the great extra weight on the crossing piers of the new central tower. Poised above the actual crossing is the delicate fan-vault of the tower, sparingly touched with colour. To the north and south the transepts end in great Perpendicular windows. These are partly filled, as is the west window, with some of the superb twelfth-century figures of patriarchs which were once in the choir (the figures now there being reproductions). In addition they have some more silvery glass of the fifteenth century, the northern window containing the praying figures of Edward IV with his wife and family, among them the princes done to death in the Tower. Here in the north transept, before the altar of St Benedict, Becket fell, but little remains from that time save perhaps the flagstones and the transept's name, 'The Martyrdom', which has persisted from before the Reformation. Opening out from it is the fan-vaulted Lady Chapel of about 1450, of great beauty for its general planning and detail but very small for such a chapel in an English cathedral. Corresponding to it on the south side the slightly earlier St Michael's, or Warrior, Chapel has a fine lierne vault and is crowded with monuments, most notably that of its builder Lady Margaret Holland (d. 1439) and her two husbands. From the central crossing flights of steps ascend to the choir which is entered through a fine early fifteenth-century screen built on to the front of that erected about 1320 by Prior Eastry who also put up the stone screens enclosing the actual choir.

Before visiting the choir and its eastward extensions one should see the crypts. These largely reproduce the ground plan of the work above them, but the larger of the two successive crypts, the Norman work of Ernulph and Conrad, retains its completely apsidal termination and thus indicates the plan of the cathedral's eastern limb as Becket would have known it. This western portion of the crypt has a fine, unusual series of Romanesque carved capitals and ornamented pillars, being lit now by windows inserted late in the fifteenth century. In the undercroft of the south-eastern transept, now used for French Protestant services, is the Black Prince's large chantry, the double chapel having been refashioned and newly vaulted in the early Perpendicular style. The crypt of St Anselm's Chapel has its own little lower chapel of St Gabriel, preserving mural paintings which give some idea of the mediaeval splendour of this lower church, with its glimmering altars and chantries. At the end of its middle aisle is the particularly beautiful Chapel of Our Lady in Crypta, screened in with Perpendicular stonework and once containing the fabulous treasure which was described by Erasmus and was only revealed to privileged eyes. The eastern crypt beneath the Trinity Chapel and Corona, with its paired cylindrical piers and a central row of Purbeck marble vaulting pillars, is a beautiful little church in itself, and belongs to the early Gothic building whose high elevation above the choir is due to the loftier vault of this eastern crypt.

The ill-lit choir (23), under its low, rather heavy sexpartite vault, is of great architectural interest for the way in which early Gothic arcades and upper structure, of a clearly French type, are fitted inside the lower walls of the older eastern limb. But the signs of immaturity and compromise, as compared with the neater and more finished design of the Trinity Chapel, are easily apparent, and as a finished work this choir cannot compare with its near contemporaries, St Hugh's choir at Lincoln or the nave and transepts at Wells. In the aisles, however, we may admire some of Canterbury's fine collection of early thirteenth-century glass, and in St Anselm's Chapel the surviving mid-twelfth-century wall painting of St Paul and the viper at Malta is among the most priceless treasures of English mediaeval art. The choir's canopied return stalls are magnificent Baroque woodwork, made between 1676 and 1682 by Roger Davis of London, and the brass eagle lectern of 1663 was also made in London by William Burroughes (who also cast the lecterns at Lincoln and Wells). A broad flight of steps leads up to the high altar, now deprived of its reredos which ran between the presbytery pillars where the structure cants inwards to allow for the surviving Norman chapels. In this chapel we have an apsidal ambulatory of French type around an arcade of coupled pillars whose capitals are carved in the Corinthian manner and whose main structure is of varied stones and marbles probably given by individual foreign donors. The site of Becket's shrine is behind the high altar, and close to it is a pavement of Alexandrian mosaic brought back from the East by Crusaders. At the east end the Corona forms a lofty circular chapel which contains the archaic stone chair on which the English primates are enthroned. The lancets of the Trinity Chapel, and those of the Corona, contain more of Canterbury's splendid collection of old glass, deep-toned medallion work of the early thirteenth century and perhaps from Chartres.

A whole chapter could be written on the monuments, mediaeval and later, with which the cathedral at Canterbury is crowded. The two most important, built one on each side of Becket's shrine, are those of Edward the Black Prince (d. 1376) and of King Henry IV (d. 1413). The fine, simple monument of the Black Prince(15), with its superb gilt bronze effigy and bitter Norman-French inscription, lies beneath a wooden tester bearing many traces of the original painting. Splendid modern replicas of his funeral achievements (helmet, gauntlets, surcoat, and scabbard) now hang above him, and his shield is on a pillar close by; the faded originals are now in a glass case not far away. Across the Trinity Chapel lies his son's usurper Henry IV with his second wife Joan of Navarre, while their little fan-vaulted chantry opens out, behind a wooden screen, from the aisle beside the tomb. Elsewhere in the eastern limb are the tombs of many mediaeval archbishops; those of Mepeham (d. 1333), Chichele (d. 1443), and Cardinal Kemp (d. 1454) are of special note. Many later archbishops, including modern holders of the primacy, are also commemorated in various ways, while the Renaissance monument to the Elizabethan Dean Nicholas Wotton is a fine combination of figure sculpture, symbolism, and architectural design. Other deans, most notably Dean Boys (d. 1625), have memorials in the Lady Chapel; this and the Warrior Chapel with its fine Baroque monument to Admiral Rooke, the captor of Gibraltar, are an epitome of English funeral craft at its best. The monuments in the transepts and nave are mostly to soldiers and seamen, and American visitors will note with interest that within a few feet of where Becket died there is a simple mural to a naval officer who was captured in the fiercest and most epic of the sea fights of Paul Jones. More notable, in the nave's north aisle, is Nicholas Stone's delightful little mural monument, with a portrait bust, to the famous composer Orlando Gibbons, who died in 1625.

The remains of the conventual buildings are too extensive for adequate description here, but mention must be made of the ruined arcade, chapel, and miniature cloister of the infirmary, the interesting circular Norman 'water-tower', or conduit, and the Norman staircase further out in the Close. The early Perpendicular cloisters are somewhat dilapidated, but have had the profuse heraldry of their bosses most beautifully repainted. The chapter-house is in good condition, a large, spacious, rectangular room reconstructed, above its lower walls, by Prior Chillenden, with large windows and a painted wooden ceiling.

CARLISLE
The Cathedral Church of the Holy and Undivided Trinity

This cathedral stands pleasantly, amid the green patches of its Close, on high ground at the upper end of the old city and not far from the castle. Though only its 'head and shoulders' survive there is much in the building to command admiration, and in the great east window we have a supreme achievement of mature Gothic art. The first church was begun by Walter, a Norman priest whom William Rufus had appointed governor of the town. It was completed by Henry I who endowed a priory of Augustinian canons to serve it. The church was finished in 1123, and from what remains of its nave and transepts it would seem that its fabric was of the architectural modesty which was typical of the early Augustinian churches as compared with the more imposing churches of the Benedictine abbeys. In 1133 the priory church at Carlisle became the cathedral of the newly constituted bishopric. In the next century the Norman eastern limb was replaced by one on a larger, more obviously cathedralesque scale; as greater breadth could only be obtained by expanding northwards the new choir was out of line with the nave. Minor fires soon caused some alterations; these disasters culminated in 1292 in a destructive blaze which only spared the vaulted aisles of the choir. This fire brought about the fourteenth-century transformation, and the creation of a choir of the utmost splendour and beauty. After the siege of 1645 the domestic buildings of the dissolved cathedral priory were largely demolished by the Scottish troops to make new fortifications, and six bays of the decayed nave were pulled down at about the same time. In the '45, Jacobite prisoners who were herded into the building did further damage. It is, however, a matter of great satisfaction that despite vicissitudes, and despite much restoration by Ewan Christian in the 1850s, the cathedral keeps so many of its excellent old fittings.

Of the Norman nave, sternly designed with its plain cylindrical pillars, triforium arcades, and slightly more ornate clerestory, only a fragment of two bays remains; the pillars of the third bay are built into the two heavy western buttresses. The façades of the two transepts are modern reconstructions. The Norman crossing piers have good scalloped capitals, and when Bishop Strickland built the simple early Perpendicular tower about 1401 he took down the Norman tower arches, and above their piers installed the piers of his own new tower arches; the northern one of these has a strainer arch in the manner of Salisbury, with tracery above it to give a more artistic effect. Returning to the exterior, we find that the contrast between the grey severity of the nave and the lightness of the choir is enhanced by the use in the latter of a pleasant red sandstone which is now (1960) undergoing much renewal. The few Perpendicular windows inserted in the choir aisles have been replaced by modern lancets, but the Decorated clerestory windows afford a contrast in the diversity of their flowing tracery. The east end is a graceful, dignified composition, almost filled by the great curvilinear window of nine lights which is the cathedral's great glory; a smaller, triangular window is in the gable above.

Inside, more Norman work is seen in the south transept, from which a Norman arch leads into the little Chapel of St Catherine. This is of unaltered Early English architecture and is enclosed by Prior Gondebour's fretted and flamboyant screen of the late fifteenth century, among the most exquisite in England in the lacelike delicacy of its detail. The choir aisles are of thirteenth-century design, with certain differences of detail in their vaulting and wall

arcades; profuse dogtooth decoration adorns the cinquefoiled arcading in the northern aisle. As the
choir was lengthened in the fourteenth century by one eastern bay,
the chapel at the end of each aisle
is clearly Decorated in style. Except
for this one bay, the main choir
arcades retain their thirteenth-
century arches with dogtooth orna-
· ment. Beneath them, after the fire of
1292, the fourteenth-century masons
skilfully inserted new piers and recut
the capitals with a display of
naturalistic carving; the subjects of
this fine sculpture include scenes
appropriate to each month of the
year. The Decorated triforium is
delicately treated in trios of two-light
curvilinear openings, and the clerestory windows, likewise curvilinear,

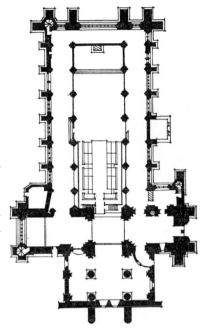

rise above a parapet of pierced quatrefoils. The great east window (24) is a
masterpiece, in Rickman's words, 'by far the most free and brilliant example
of Decorated tracery in the kingdom'; it is comparable, to its advantage, only
with the west window at York. The glass of its main lights is modern, but
that in the tracery is contemporary with the window and is very beautiful. The
choir is roofed by a timber barrel-roof from which non-structural hammer-
beams project; from 1764 for nearly a century this carpentry was hidden by a
Georgian Gothic plaster vault of simple design. The canopied stalls only
partly back onto the late mediaeval screen because the narrowness of the
Norman tower arch only makes a screen necessary across part of the opening
into the choir. The canopied stalls themselves are of sound fifteenth-century
work, with misericords whose subjects give a good section of the mediaeval
Bestiary; behind them, and well seen in the aisles, are some crude but
interesting paintings which show scenes from the life of St Cuthbert and,
very fittingly in a church of Austin canons, from those of St Anthony
Abbot and St Augustine. More sophisticated is the beautiful Renaissance
screen of Lancelot Salkeld (25), the last prior; he was the cathedral's first dean

by the time that he set up the screen, with the badge of the Five Wounds and the arms of Henry VIII, about 1542. Modern screenwork of great distinction, erected in 1949 to designs by Mr Stephen Dykes Bower, is seen in the nave. Despite earlier projects, there are now no immediate plans for rebuilding this nave to its original size, and it has been beautifully fitted up as the Memorial Chapel of the Border Regiment.

The canons' domestic buildings were largely rebuilt in the fifteenth century, but most of them have now been demolished. There remains, however, a large and splendid refectory over a fourteenth-century undercroft. It has Decorated windows on one side and Perpendicular on the other, and is now used as a chapter-house and cathedral library. At the upper end is the attractive little reader's pulpit, with a staircase ceiled by cusped circles.

The monuments in the cathedral are not of much note, though the Georgian murals to Bishop Fleming (d. 1747) and by Banks to Bishop Law (d. 1787) are worth a glance. Much better, however, are the fine canopied brass to Bishop Bell (d. 1496) and an engraved brass plate to Bishop Robinson (d. 1616) which is a contemporary replica of one at Queen's College, Oxford, of which the bishop was provost.

Carlisle Cathedral has one good literary association, for Sir Walter Scott was married there in 1797.

CHESTER

The Cathedral Church of Christ and the Blessed Virgin Mary

The Benedictine abbey of St Werburga at Chester was founded in 1093 by Hugh Lupus, Earl of Chester and Lord of the Welsh Marches. Its church was made a cathedral by Henry VIII and is attractive in retaining many furnishings which were familiar to its former occupants. But the monastic buildings far exceed in interest the remodelled, drastically refaced, and pedantically renovated church. The cathedral's peculiar plan was the outcome of its position in a small walled city, whose north-eastern corner it occupied with little room for expansion. When it became necessary to

26 *Chester from the south-east. Choir designed by Richard Lenginour, c. 1283–1315; south transept partly fourteenth century; tower Perpendicular*

27 *Chester: the entrance canopy and return stalls of the choir, c. 1390*

28 Chichester from the south. Upper stage of south-west tower 1215–25; south transept 1305–36. Central tower and spire rebuilt on old lines 1861–66, by Sir Giles Gilbert Scott

29 Chichester: the nave, 1114–48, looking east. Vaulting and recasing 1187–99, by Walter of Coventry

30 Chichester: the Transitional design of the retrochoir, 1187–99, by Walter of Coventry

enlarge it, the cloisters precluded development to the north and the city to the west. Thus the lengthening proceeded east and then south, taking in the parish church of St Oswald which was adapted as a large, double-aisled transept of five bays. The monks built the lay congregation a new church outside their precincts, but this has now been destroyed. The disputes entailed by these incidents continued throughout the Middle Ages and beyond the Reformation.

The cathedral at Chester is built of red sandstone and the fabric has suffered much, at all periods, from the friable nature of this material. Of the founder's church the surviving portions are the lower stages of the north-western tower (with simple arches and scalloped capitals), the outer wall of the nave's north aisle, and the north transept with its range of crude triforium arches. The first great period of new building was in the thirteenth and early fourteenth centuries. A new Lady Chapel was built and the eastern limb was gradually remodelled. Then in the fourteenth century the monks set about enlargements which included the huge south transept (the largest transept in any English cathedral) and the first stages of the new nave and central tower (26). Work was, however, interrupted by the Black Death and was not resumed till late in the fifteenth century, when the design was modified and some work of a different character was done under Abbots Simon Ripley (1485–1498) and Birkenshaw (1498–1537); the west front built by the last named is of a decidedly early Tudor type. Many of the Perpendicular windows put into various parts of the cathedral during this last period were replaced, under Sir Gilbert Scott in the nineteenth century, by Victorian Decorated windows whose tracery was assumed to be in accordance with the design as originally conceived. The frames, however, and the exterior gables are often the originals. Much of the vaulting, including the wooden vault of the nave, is also modern work.

The cathedral's interior is warm and mellow in tone, with some fine effects of lighting. There is, however, a certain gauntness about the nave, a two-storeyed structure with no triforium, but with a footwalk running below the clerestory windows. The well-proportioned north arcade is slightly richer in detail than the earlier one on the southern side, but in their general design the two arcades are closely assimilated. The Norman north transept has seen many changes, for it was once screened off by a heavy stone screen, and the arch to its eastern chapel, now opened out, was at one time blocked up.

The choir was gradually rebuilt in the late thirteenth and early fourteenth

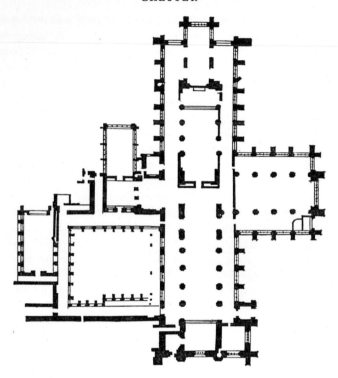

centuries, and changes of design can be noticed as one looks at the pillars and arches from east to west. This choir, like the nave, is virtually of two storeys, with blind trefoil-headed arcading instead of a triforium and a passageway, set back behind a parapet of pierced quatrefoils, round the clerestory windows. The woodwork of the choir (27), moved several times from its original position below the tower, is the cathedral's chief glory, and the stalls are among the very finest in England. This canopied and pinnacled stallwork remains largely as executed except for the front pillars which have been cut away so as to impair the upward effect of the design. It was erected about 1380, some ten years after the stallwork at Lincoln on which it is an improvement. The stalls retain their superb series of misericords illustrating fables, scriptural scenes, and incidents from the mediaeval Bestiaries. The entrance to the choir preserves its mass of pinnacled detail, but the stone *pulpitum* has been removed.

The choir aisles end in chapels of differing character; the northern chapel is now Perpendicular, and one bay of it overlaps the fine thirteenth-century Lady Chapel with its lancets, double piscina, and splendid carved bosses of which one shows the martyrdom of St Thomas Becket. The weird 'candle-snuffer' roof over the south-eastern chapel was designed by Sir Gilbert Scott. The fourteenth-century shrine of St Werburga is now preserved in the Lady Chapel.

The renovated cloister, with its windows now glazed, diffuses a feeling of continuity and use, and is a centre of cathedral and diocesan activity. The garth is now a flower garden, from the centre of which the monastery tank has been excavated; this was originally served with water by means of lead pipes from Christleton, two miles away. As one leaves the cathedral by its north-eastern processional doorway, the first doorway on the right leads to the chapter-house vestibule whose thirteenth-century vault, like that of the parlour further on, is supported on slender columns entirely without capitals. The Early English chapter-house is rectangular in plan, with tall lancet windows which have a footwalk at the level of their sills. A cupboard here incorporates the fine scroll ironwork of Thomas de Leighton who was also responsible for the grille before the tomb of Queen Eleanor in Westminster Abbey, and the door ironwork of Eaton Bray church in Bedfordshire.

Continuing from the chapter-house we pass the slype which led to the infirmary and monks' cemetery; through the next trefoil-headed stairway are the day stairs which once went up to the destroyed dormitory. In the cloister's northern range we find the remains of the monks' *lavatorium*, with the entrance to the refectory immediately beyond it. This fine room, long used as a classroom by the Grammar School, was also at one time cut short by a dean to make a convenient passage from his house to the cathedral. It has now been restored to its full length and is used for meetings. Dating from the thirteenth century it retains its beautiful pulpit from which readings were given during the monks' meals, the only others of its type in anything like a complete state being at Beaulieu and Shrewsbury.

The passage adjoining the refectory led to the kitchens. Turning left, we enter the western cloister alley, bounded by the fine Norman undercroft which was originally partitioned as cellarage space. Above it was the abbot's lodging, but all that remains of this is the Norman chapel, enlarged and refitted by Bishop Bridgeman in the seventeenth century, which overhangs the cloister at its south-western corner. In this western cloister walk are the carrels which once made small closets for study. The southern alleyway, rebuilt by Scott, also has carrels, and Norman round-arched recesses line its inner wall which is also that of the church's north aisle.

The monuments in Chester cathedral are of no great note except for some of Baroque design at the west end of the nave; these include one to a senior Royalist officer who was killed at the siege of Chester in 1644. A better feature is the Renaissance font of black marble.

CHICHESTER
The Cathedral Church of the Holy Trinity

For its setting Chichester Cathedral has one of the most charming old towns in England, lying in the flat country of West Sussex between the wooded South Downs and the English Channel; it is the only one of England's pre-Reformation cathedrals which is visible from the sea. Moderate in size, it stands in a narrow strip of green churchyard, with a cluster of old canonical houses on the south side; of these the most attractive are the early Georgian deanery and the much-altered Vicars' Close, laid out on the same lines as were Calendarhay at Exeter and Vicars' Close at Wells, with a hall of the Perpendicular period over a splendid vaulted undercroft of about 1200 which is now a restaurant.

The cathedral, like Hereford, was one served by secular canons which all through the Middle Ages retained the basically Norman character of its design. The exterior (*28*), however, shows the somewhat heterogeneous nature of the fabric, most of it built between 1091 and 1305. The former date approximately marks the beginning of the Norman church under Bishop Ralph de Luffa soon after the move of the see from Selsey. Its dedication took place about twenty years later, though it is doubtful how far work had by then advanced. The church was certainly complete, with its nave, at the time of the fire in 1187 which did serious damage and caused its roofing throughout with a plain stone vault which necessitated a general adjustment of the design. Another result was the remodelling of the presbytery's two eastern bays to an interesting design, in which rounded arches and Purbeck marble played an important part, under Bishop Seffrid II between 1187 and 1199. It is believed that the craftsmen employed on this work had been trained under William of Sens and William the Englishman at Canterbury, and Mr Bond regarded it admiringly as 'an Anglicised and improved version of the Canterbury choir, though still retaining traces of French influence, as in the square abacus and the foliated capitals of piers and shafts'. The lateral nave chapels date in part from the later thirteenth century, and the Lady Chapel was lengthened by two bays, and partially remodelled in three more, under Bishop Gilbert de Leophardi (1288–1305). The first stone spire was raised over the central tower by Bishop Rede about 1380.

The west front, with its projecting Galilee of the thirteenth century, is flanked by somewhat gaunt towers which once had short spires. The lower stages of these are Norman and the upper Early English; the northern one, which collapsed about 1635, is largely a modern copy of the older work. On the same side, a mere stone's throw away, is a plain detached campanile, with a turreted lantern storey, which was built in the fifteenth century to reduce the load on the central tower. The seven-light, much restored curvilinear window in the south transept is very fine, with a small rose window in the gable above it, while the east end also has its rose window above a trio of lancets flanked by pointed turrets. The central tower is surmounted by a tall spire, a competent rebuilding of the original, already repaired by Wren, which collapsed in 1861. The series of lateral chapels south and north of the nave almost form a second pair of complete aisles, the extra altar space needed in a cathedral of the Middle Ages being provided here rather than by the building of extra transepts at the east end. The south side is screened by an irregularly shaped cloister, one of whose walks leads to the thirteenth-century 'St Richard's' porch by which the bishops were provided, as at Lincoln, with a splendid entrance to the cathedral from their palace. These cloisters have unglazed Perpendicular windows and a mediocre timber waggon-roof; they were intended as no more than a covered approach to the church for the canons and vicars choral. At the east end the Lady Chapel forms a narrow extension lit by tall windows with varied Geometrical tracery.

Inside, the nave (29) is built to a close-knit, simple Norman design with square piers more like sections of wall than pillars. This severity is relieved by the simple, effective treatment of the triforium in coupled, round-headed openings within containing arches, and with an interesting variety of incised patterns in the spandrels of the four western bays. The design was also much modified, at the time when the early Gothic vault was put on, by the re-moulding of the main arches on their inner sides and by the erection, at the

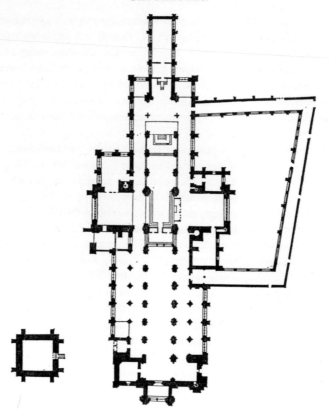

corners of the piers, of Purbeck marble shafts. In contrast to the nave's
general weight and darkness the bright vistas of the lateral chapels, with
their ample windows ranging from paired lancets to full Geometrical
designs, are very pleasing. The choir, as far as the sanctuary, continues the
architectural design of the nave, and built into the wall of its south aisle are
two remarkable Romanesque sculptured reliefs, tinged with strong Byzantine
influence and showing Christ with Martha and Mary(7) and the raising
of Lazarus. They may have come from the Saxon cathedral at Selsey, but
more probably date from about 1130–1140. The choir fittings are modern
except for the stalls, unassuming work of the fourteenth century with some
most interesting misericords; the two fine brass chandeliers were given
in 1752.

East of the high altar screen the Transitional retrochoir (*30*), once containing the feretory of St Richard (who was Bishop of Chichester from 1245 to 1253), has a most graceful design of two bays, unusual in its grouping round each central pier of four slender Purbeck shafts. The foliate carving of the capitals is advanced for its period, and the arches are round-headed yet suggestive of Early English in the incisiveness of their moulding. The triforium design, of coupled and pointed arches between clustered Purbeck shafts and within round containing arches, is of remarkable maturity and the two pairs of upper arches in the east wall are much enriched with extra carving. In the tympana of these triforium arches are recesses with carved foliage and figures of a somewhat later, thirteenth-century date. An arch in the east wall of the retrochoir leads to the Lady Chapel. Of this, the two western bays still show the simple vaulting of the Norman eastern chapel as first reconstructed about 1200, but the three eastern bays were partly refashioned and partly new built about 1300, with a fine tierceron vault and naturalistic foliate capitals as at Southwell. There are also some fine early Decorated windows, the eastern one being crudely clipped at the top by the vault. In one of the westerly vault compartments is a remnant of the floral arabesque painting carried out in 1519 by a local painter named Lambert Bernard who also, at the orders of Bishop Sherborne (1508–1535), originally did the large painted panels in the transepts. Bishop Sherborne's canopied tomb, with its beautiful effigy, is among the best of the cathedral's episcopal memorials; another fine one, within a beautiful cusped and pinnacled arcade in the south transept, is that of Bishop Stratford (1337–1362). Of the later memorials, several of the modest ones in the Baroque style commemorate bishops of the late seventeenth century, while an attractive group, with reliefs of naval battles and other nautical details, are those to naval officers of the Georgian period, arranged in the charming seamen's chapel which has recently been fitted up beneath the north-west tower. Seven of the cathedral's numerous Greek Revival monuments are by Flaxman who once lived in the district; they include a fine posthumous one to the poet William Collins, who was born in Chichester and there died sadly in 1759.

The fine Perpendicular stone screen, erected by Bishop Arundel (1459–1477), which was discarded from the entrance to the choir not long before the spire fell in 1861, has been partially rebuilt in the detached belfry. Fortunately a scheme is now on foot to reinstate it in its proper position.

DURHAM

The Cathedral Church of Christ and the Blessed Virgin Mary

Durham is the most impressively situated of all English cathedrals; the grouping of its towers above the steep wooded slopes of the Wear(*31*) provides one of the most memorable views in the country. But apart from the beauty of its surroundings the church itself has a strong appeal: to the architect as the first example of ribbed stone vaulting on a grand scale, to the religious-minded as enshrining the names of Cuthbert and Bede, and to everyone for the romance of its origin and the stern dignity of its fabric. St Cuthbert, whose early days were spent as a shepherd boy near Melrose, was a member of the evangelising brotherhood of Iona. Between long periods of solitude he emerged first as prior, and later as the unwilling bishop, of Lindisfarne, the Holy Island off the Northumbrian coast from which the first conversion of Northern England was largely effected. Here he died and was buried in 687. But his remains were not long left undisturbed, for with the incursions of Danes and Norsemen, and with the increasing insecurity of Northumbria, they were moved from Lindisfarne and launched on over a century of intermittent wandering. Each resting place was marked by a church dedicated to the saint, and it was not until 995 that the brothers 'with great Joy arrived with his Body at Dunholme', where, impressed with the strength of this rocky plateau surrounded on three sides by the river, they raised a 'little Church of Wands and Branches' where the cathedral now stands. In 998 Aldhelm completed the first stone church where the shrine rested till 1091 when the second Norman bishop William of St Carileph laid the foundations of a new church for the Benedictines; the eastern limb of this was ready by 1104. The nave was continued under Flambard and the whole structure, including the stone vaults over all its sections, was finished in 1133. Thus, during a period of some forty years, every part of the cathedral was roofed with rib vaulting as the first master had planned, and to sustain the thrust the piers were strengthened by arches or flying buttresses at triforium level under the aisle roofs.

In its strength and grandeur the Anglo-Norman building that emerged remains unsurpassed. Its plan was typical of the Benedictine arrangement, and, except for the choir vault which had to be rebuilt in the thirteenth

66

31 *Durham from the south-west, above the River Wear. Upper stages of western towers* c. *1220; lower stage of central tower 1465–75, upper stage* c. *1483–90, by John Bell, junior*

32 *Durham: west end of the nave, showing Bishop Cosin's font and canopy, installed soon after the Restoration. Nave 1099–1128; nave vault 1128–33*

33 *Durham: the late Norman arcades of the Galilee, c. 1170, by Richard Wolveston*

century, the work of the Norman builders continues in the main unaltered throughout the fabric; one must, however, remember that the present Norman, round-arched appearance of many of the windows is due to their 're-Normanisation' by the Victorian destruction of Perpendicular mullions and tracery which had been inserted into the frames. Some of these windows now have excellent modern glass by Mr Hugh Easton whose style is well suited to their unimpeded, untraceried expanses. The main replacement of Norman work has been at the east end where the final bay of the choir and the Chapel of the Nine Altars are important thirteenth-century additions. The twin western towers are Norman to the level of the nave clerestory, and were then raised in the Early English period. At one time they both had spires, and their present battlements and pinnacles were added in the first half of last century. They compose magnificently with the lofty splendour of the central tower which was built about 1465–1490; from the west, as one looks across the river and up the steep, dense slopes to the church, an impression of great height adds to their quiet dignity. Abutting on the west front is the remarkable Galilee chapel placed as a kind of narthex which screens the entrance to the cathedral and was added about 1175 by Bishop Puiset, a nephew of King Stephen. It was built as a Lady Chapel, and is an exception to the normal rule that this chapel should be east of the presbytery. Its actual position was reputedly due to the intervention of St Cuthbert, whose ineradicable aversion to women expressed itself in some structural failures when the work was begun in the usual position adjoining his shrine. The building is an exquisite creation of the late twelfth century, divided into five aisles by arcades of rich chevron arches and lit by Decorated and Perpendicular windows which are later insertions. But, though the masons produced a beautiful if somewhat archaic design, they lacked technical skill and the structure had to be much strengthened under Cardinal Langley (1406–1437) by the building of massive and lofty buttresses to prevent it from sliding down towards the river.

The nave (32) presents one of the finest Romanesque interiors in Europe. Its arcades were built in pairs of arches, the great transverse arches of the vault rising up between each main compartment. These arches were slightly pointed, and photographs show how the fashion for pointed arches arose from this constructional device. Massive cylindrical columns (2), adorned with a variety of bold chiselled patterns, alternate with the clustered shafting of the main supporting piers, and the billet and chevron motifs are effectively used on the arch-moulds and vaulting ribs. The same design continues in the transepts and in the Norman part of the choir. Beyond the choir, the transeptal Chapel of the Nine Altars was added in the thirteenth century to replace the original Norman apses. The work was begun under Prior Melsanby in 1242 and the master mason was Richard of Farnham whose head, in a close-fitting cap, is carved on the wall arcade. It was a happy idea, already carried out with notable success at Fountains Abbey, and, although the work was so slowly done that the later windows are of Geometrical design and not Early English lancets, it resulted in one of the most notable works of its time. Here was lodged the shrine of St Cuthbert, and a fine modern painted tester now hangs above the feretory. The *Rites of Durham* vividly describes the famous mediaeval tomb 'exalted with the most curious workmanship, of fine and costly green marble, all limned and gilt with gold . . . the cover of the shrine being wainscot . . . to which six very fine-sounding bells were fastened which stirred all men's hearts that were in the church to repair unto it. On either side of the said cover were painted four lively images, curiously wrought and miraculous to all beholders thereof. Also within the feretory . . . were almeries, varnished and finely painted and gilt over with fine little images, for the relics belonging to St Cuthbert to lie in; all the costly reliques and jewels that hung about within the said feretory upon the irons being accounted the most sumptuous and rich jewels in all this land.'

Between the feretory platform and the high altar stands the great stone screen, erected in 1372 as the gift of John, Lord Nevile of Raby. It is made of Dorset stone, was worked in London, and was brought to Newcastle by sea. It contained 107 alabaster figures in its beautifully pinnacled niches; these included Our Lady, St Cuthbert, and St Oswald. The work is continued on either side of the sanctuary to form sedilia. On the south side of the choir stands the lofty stepped throne made about 1375 by order of Bishop Thomas Hatfield. Below it is the bishop's chantry, and behind the actual chair on its elevated platform is delicate tabernacle work like that of the Nevile screen. The richly carved wooden stairway balustrade was given about 1700 by Bishop Lord Crewe, and the whole composition is worthy of the Palatine see and its prince-bishops. In 1650 the mediaeval choir stalls were destroyed by Scottish prisoners captured at Dunbar and confined in the cathedral. Soon after 1660 they were replaced by Bishop Cosin of happy memory. The stalls then inserted are magnificently canopied in the fifteenth-century manner, but mixed with their predominantly mediaeval idiom one notices such Renaissance details as Ionic pillarets and winged cherubs' heads. Still more Renaissance detail, particularly in the main pillars and in

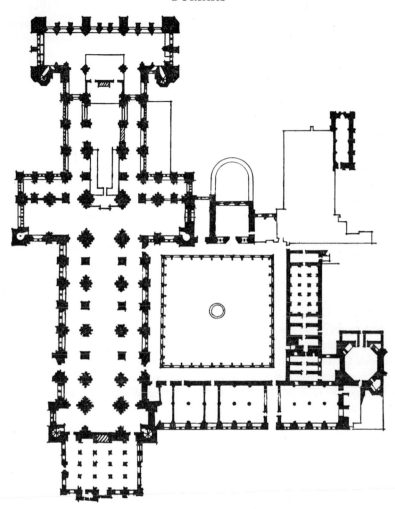

its Baroque cartouches, is blended with late Gothic design in the towering pinnacled canopy which encloses and surmounts Cosin's white marble font in the nave (*32*). But Cosin's great *pulpitum* was demolished by the Victorian Salvin, and a poorly designed marble Gothic screen by Scott was substituted. The shrine of the Venerable Bede was in 1370 encased in plates of gold and silver, and placed in the Galilee (*33*) where Bede's bones still lie under a plain tomb.

Durham Cathedral suffered drastically at the hands of Wyatt who chiselled two inches of stone off the fabric's exterior, substituted a weakly designed rose window for the one which previously adorned the east end, and was only just prevented from pulling down the Galilee to make a western carriage drive. Nevertheless the cathedral is fortunate in retaining most of its monastic buildings, though Prior Washington's fifteenth-century cloister has been considerably altered and the fine Norman chapter-house, whose apsidal east end was demolished by Wyatt to make the room more cosy for the canons, has been rebuilt in a form akin to the original. The refectory (on its fine Norman undercroft) was rebuilt as a library in 1662–1684; south of it the octagonal prior's kitchen, ingeniously vaulted and with a central louvre to emit the smoke, is like the one at Glastonbury. The whole west side of the monastic buildings is occupied by the great dormitory, built between 1398 and 1404 over an earlier undercroft and with small windows, below its main ones, to light the monks' cubicles. It is 194 feet long and still has its crudely massive roof of oak trunks hardly touched by the axe. It is now a museum, and its contents include a priceless collection of Celtic and early Saxon crosses from the neighbourhood.

Durham Cathedral is not rich in monuments. One should, however, notice in the Nine Altars' Chapel the pleasing Adamesque tablet to Dean Spencer Cowper (d. 1774) and the imposing seated statue of Bishop van Mildert (d. 1836), the last of Durham's prince-bishops and the founder of the University which now occupies their castle and many others among the buildings enclosed by the great loop in the river Wear.

∽∾∽∾∽∾∽∾

ELY

The Cathedral Church of the Holy and Undivided Trinity

The ecclesiastical history of Ely begins in 673. In that year Etheldreda, an East Anglian princess who is said to have retained her virginity though twice married, founded a religious house on land she had obtained from her first husband. She assigned to the new foundation her entire principality in the Isle of Ely; this endowment formed the nucleus of the cathedral priory's mediaeval wealth. About two centuries later the establishment was sacked by the Danes and its religious were mostly put to death. But a few survivors

34   Ely: the nave, 1090–1130, looking towards the Octagon

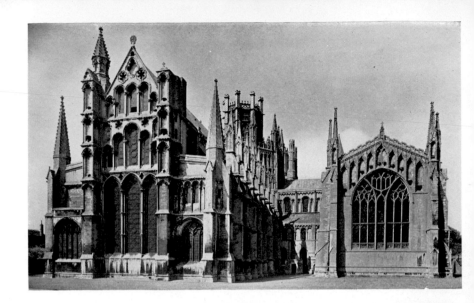

35 Ely: the east end,
c. 1240–50, and the
Lady Chapel, 1321–
49, adjoining the north
transept

36 Ely: the west tower
and   south-western
transept,   1174–97;
lantern c. 1392

returned, creeping back a few years later to effect a partial restoration of
the church which was then served for about a hundred years by secular
clergy. About 970, in the reign of King Edgar and at the time of the great
Benedictine revival which transformed other religious houses elsewhere,
rehabilitation came to Ely on a large scale. Benedictine monks were introduced, extra endowments were given, the monks' ownership of the Isle
was confirmed by royal charter, and the abbey became one of great
wealth.

During the resistance to William the Conqueror by Hereward the Wake
the fabric of the Saxon church suffered little or no damage at the besiegers'
hands. Its complete rebuilding, started by Abbot Simeon in 1083, is part of
the general movement at that time to erect larger, more magnificent churches
which would both glorify God and enhance the prestige of the Benedictines.
The presbytery was probably the first part of the new church to be started,
and has been replaced by later work. It was finished by 1106, and the
remains of the canonised foundress, together with those of her sister St
Sexburga and of her companions St Ermenilda and St Withburga,
were then ceremonially reburied before the high altar. The transepts had
probably been started by this time, and they are the oldest part of the present
building. In 1109 the abbey became the cathedral church of the newly
created diocese. The building of the nave and the reconstruction of the
monastic buildings continued through most of the twelfth century. Of
Bishop Riddell (1174–1189) we read that 'he carried on the new work, and
the tower and the west end of the new church, almost to the top'. The
beautiful Galilee porch, projecting from the west wall of the western tower,
was at least partially built in the early years of the thirteenth century by
Bishop Eustace (1198–1215). The upper stages of the west tower were added
a little later, and this tower was originally capped by a stone spire. These
operations bring us to the time of Bishop Northwold (1229–1254), and
his period saw the demolition of the eastern part of the Norman choir and
the building of the cathedral's present easternmost part; the result was that
the whole building was considerably lengthened. Except for the beginning
of the present Lady Chapel, in an unusual position to the north-east of the
cathedral, no major work was undertaken before 1323 when the Norman
central tower crashed down and destroyed three bays of the church's
eastern limb.

This disaster gave his opportunity to Alan of Walsingham, the sacrist of
the cathedral priory and therefore the man responsible for planning and

organising any building programme that might become necessary. Though various masons had to do much of the detailed design work, it is quite possible that Walsingham was responsible for the general idea of building the splendid octagon, with its timber lantern rising above the great space so created, which was now built to replace the fallen tower. The carpentry of the lantern was, however, supervised by William Hurley, a man at that time of special eminence in his profession. The three western bays of the choir were also rebuilt at this period, and the magnificent Lady Chapel was continued under Walsingham's guidance, though not finished till about the middle of the fourteenth century.

Ely itself, on its eminence of firm ground looking out over the Fens, has a somewhat abstracted, sleepy air—except for Southwell and Wells it is the smallest episcopal city in England. Its large parish church of St Mary, and the old houses of the Close are, however, full of interest. The red brick Palace (now used as a Red Cross school) is partly early Tudor and partly in the Wren style. The precincts are entered from the south through Ely Porta, a large stone gatehouse built late in the fourteenth century. The open green in front of the cathedral adds much to the effect of the west front (*36*), a most striking composition, originally having western transepts on each side of the tower. It derives from the idea of the *westwerk* which was a common terminating feature of several large Romanesque churches of the Rhineland and the adjoining parts of the German Empire. When first completed, with its arcading and with its full complement of turrets, this design, like the even larger one at Bury St Edmunds, must have been one of the most spectacular of its time; any effect of flatness was soon countered by the westward building of the Galilee, originally with an entrance simpler than the present traceried Victorian work. In the shapes of their arches, in their incised decoration, and in the carving of some of the capitals, these tiers of closely ranged arcading which pattern the faces of the western transepts and tower clearly show the process of development from round-arched Romanesque, through Transitional, to early Gothic with its lancets. The tower was completed in the fourteenth century by adding a lantern storey with octagonal corner turrets, which, till 1801, was crowned by a lightly built, slender spire. The surviving western transept ends in two large polygonal turrets.

The external elevations of the nave show a plain, unornamented Norman fabric. The two lower ranges of windows are Perpendicular work of the fifteenth century. On the south side is the Prior's doorway with its richly carved shafts and tympanum. Adjoining the north transept is the great fourteenth-century Lady Chapel(35), in itself a brilliant masterpiece which shows niches and pinnacles of the Decorated period, and window tracery which is most of it Decorated but in some windows marks the transition from Decorated to Perpendicular. The octagonal lantern(37) over the crossing is best seen from a distance; one has to remember that its large crocketed pinnacles were added in recent years. The Norman transepts have later windows in their gables, and both are of interest in having Renaissance architectural features, a rarity in our mediaeval cathedrals since Inigo Jones made alterations to Old St Paul's. The doorway which adjoins the south transept, and leads to the surviving portion of the cloisters, is of a comparatively simple type. More Baroque in feeling is the larger doorway inserted into the north transept. This was designed in 1699 by the Cambridge architect Robert Grumbold, but Wren too was consulted, and the alterations made to the window above make it like those which Wren put into the new library at Trinity College. The cathedral's eastern limb is of a graceful, much altered thirteenth-century design. Most of its triforium windows were replaced by larger, more elaborate ones of Decorated design. Only two bays on the outer side retain, as blank and unglazed spaces, the original lancets built under Bishop Northwold, the inner triforium openings having been made into windows to throw more light onto the high altar.

As we traverse the cathedral's interior from the west end we find that the simply designed Norman nave(34) is one of the finest in England. It is also one of the latest, for it was not completed till late in the twelfth century; the moulded arches of the arcades are obviously later than the more austere ones in the somewhat older transepts. As at Norwich, the unusual height of the triforium, and the insertion of the two tiers of later windows, produce unusually full lighting for the interior; but, as one looks upwards, the dignity of the effect is diminished by the canted wooden ceiling, jammed down incongruously like a lid over the clerestory and hardly improved in itself by the nineteenth-century paintings of Styleman Le Strange and Gambier Parry. The nave terminates westward in a tremendous Perpendicular arch—a recasing of the original Norman work to strengthen the tower. The south-west transept is used as a baptistry, and out of it runs the apsed Chapel of St Catherine which is a scholarly Norman reconstruction of about 1860 by Professor Willis.

The transepts are lofty and well lit, and are the only part of any major English cathedral to have open hammerbeam roofs of the fifteenth century.

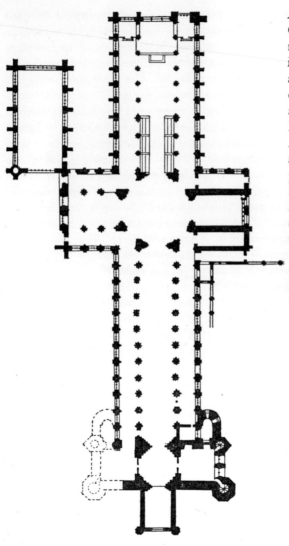

At the crossing the Octagon (*38*) remains the most daring and original architectural and constructional achievement of the English Middle Ages. Four lofty arches, on clustered piers, rise to the full height of the nave and transepts; the eastern arch is higher than the choir vault, so the space between them had to be filled with rich stone panelling. The sides of the Octagon between these great arches are filled by arches leading into the aisles, by short canopied niches, and by four great windows with curvilinear tracery. From capitals on the main piers spring eight segments of timber vaulting, the spreading ribs of which are yoked by an octagonal collar from which rises the upper lantern with its ring of windows. To carry out such an undertaking in timber during the fourteenth century was a structural achievement of the first magnitude, and it is not surprising to find that twelve years were needed for its completion. The

length and breadth of England were ransacked for oaks of sufficient scantling
—it would be ransacked in vain nowadays. The hidden beams which support
the lantern are 63 feet long and about three feet square, and the roads and
bridges leading to Ely had to be strengthened for their transportation. Today,
despite the efforts of Victorian decorators, the hideousness of its modern
Gothic metal screen, and the nightmare of its Victorian glass, the Ely
Octagon remains a work of fascinating loveliness and precision. Its lighting
effect is unforgettable, forming a luminous pool in the centre of the church
which contrasts with the deep chiaroscuro of the arcades.

Beyond Scott's screen, the first three bays of the choir represent the
fourteenth-century reconstruction made necessary by the tower's collapse.
They are of florid work, with a lavish use of cusping and rosettes, and they
are covered by a lierne vault. It is not easy to pass judgment on this somewhat
florid work as a whole, for the arcades are now almost entirely concealed
by the fine, though modernised, stalls, and an ungainly Victorian organ
sprawls over the northern triforium. The six remaining presbytery bays were
rebuilt by Bishop Northwold about 1240 to an effective design, with richly
carved foliage between the main shafts of the triforium arches, and with
large carved corbels which anticipate those later set up at Exeter. The
influence of this choir at Ely is also apparent on the later and more sumptuous
Angel Choir at Lincoln. The two chantry chapels which occupy the east
end of each choir aisle are among the most fulsome expressions of waning
English Gothic. Bishop Alcock's chapel (10) on the northern side dates from
1488, and in its elaborate profusion of canopy work and other carving
recalls the final phase of flamboyant Spanish or French Gothic. Bishop
West's chantry on the southern side, dating from 1534, has a delicacy and
restraint which is more consistent with our English Perpendicular. The
magnificent panelled ceiling, described by Celia Fiennes as 'one entire
stone most delicately carv'd in great poynts', is definitely Renaissance in
treatment, as also is the arabesque panel over the entrance which has a
beautiful and florid wrought iron gate.

The Lady Chapel (1321–1353) was built as an aisleless hall, with most
of its windows curvilinear, a broad lierne vault, and niches round the walls;
of these last the ones in the spaces between the windows have bold ogee
canopies which bulge forward in addition to the normal curvature of
their outline. Beautiful as the interior still is, the appearance of this
chapel before the destruction of its numerous statues, in their setting of
rich foliate carving, must have been unforgettable; even so the canopy work

and arcading (5) remain as one of the most glorious displays of English carving.

The cathedral at Ely is notable for the excellence of the tombs of some of its mediaeval bishops, particularly those of Northwold, Kilkenny, and de Luda who died in the thirteenth century. A sad contrast appears, in the south aisle of the choir, in the many robbed matrices which once contained the superb cross brasses of monastic priors. In St Edmund's Chapel, off the north transept, are some good wall paintings showing the kingly saint's martyrdom. The post-Reformation monuments of various bishops are also of some artistic note, though some are of a comparatively restrained design, without the portrait sculpture one finds in the monument of Bishop Gunning (1684). The cloisters have mostly been destroyed, but some of the monastic infirmary's arcade remains curiously embedded in the fronts of later houses in the Close. Other fragments of monastic ranges are incorporated in the schools and in the canons' houses. Fortunately the charming little Decorated chapel of Prior Crauden remains intact and is used as its chapel by King's School. Its wall canopies and foliate carving resemble that seen in the contemporary Lady Chapel.

EXETER
The Cathedral Church of St Peter

When in 1050 the see of Devon and Cornwall was transferred from Crediton to Exeter under Bishop Leofric, the monastic church of St Mary and St Peter was adapted as the new cathedral and the monks made way for secular clergy. The Saxon cathedral survived till the coming of Warelwast, the second Norman bishop, a nephew of the Conqueror and chaplain both to Rufus and Henry I. A larger building was then begun more to the west. Of this the present transeptal towers survive and give Exeter its distinctive, well-loved silhouette. In their disposition they resemble the flanking towers of some Rhineland churches and may also have owed something to those of the original cathedral at Old Sarum. Then about 1275 Walter Bronescombe, the first of a famous line of building bishops, began the Lady Chapel, in the fashion of his time, on the site of the Saxon cathedral; he also started the eastern extension of the presbytery. Except for this eastward extension, the Norman plan was followed throughout the ensuing reconstruction. The towers were retained as transepts and are thus unique in England, save those of the daughter church of Ottery St Mary a few miles away. Moreover, the north and south walls of the Norman nave were retained up to the sills, as also were the plain portions of the Norman choir walls above the arcading.* Peter Quivil (1280–1291) continued the work, and under Thomas Bytton (1292–1307) the presbytery and choir with their aisles were remodelled. Walter Stapledon (1308–1326) who followed Bytton furnished the choir, very largely out of his own pocket. Lord Treasurer of England and among the first courtiers of his period, he did much to create the 'radiantly decorative' character which is still Exeter's very individual charm; the screen, bishop's throne, rich sedilia, and the even richer reredos (which has now disappeared) all dated from his episcopate. In 1326 he was murdered by the mob while defending London for Edward II. John Grandisson (1327–1369) continued the work with enthusiasm, and under him the nave was completed and the whole was vaulted. By the end of the fourteenth century Exeter was among England's most sumptuously appointed cathedrals, with a rare and dazzling consistence in its 'luxurious spendthrift art' which has happily to a great extent been preserved.

Of grey stone in red sandstone country, the cathedral fabric, with the exception of a pair of Romanesque towers, represents a steady, continuous growth from the close of the thirteenth and throughout the fourteenth century, and is the finest surviving work of that period. The plan is symmetrical throughout the eastern limb—chapel to chapel, tower to tower, window to window, and the design has a real exuberance and charm in its display of pinnacles, striding buttresses and ranges of broad, splayed windows with an imaginative diversity of Geometrical and Decorated tracery that makes each one a new excitement (40). The west front (39) is built in three planes, with a triangular window, having its sides curved, in the gable, and a great nine-light window with complex tracery filling most of the upper wall. The entrance screen dates from the last quarter of the fifteenth century and displays in its three tiers an array of kings, popular saints, and angels under canopies whose stonework has been a good deal damaged and corroded, partly by the smoke of the Guy Fawkes night bonfires held for centuries

* Important fragments of Norman masonry, including large portions of cylindrical piers, were reused as the rubble infilling of later walls; many of these were revealed when the south side of the choir was hit by a bomb in 1942.

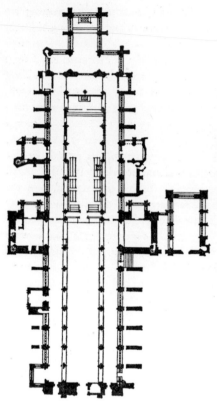

close outside. This image screen has, however, been cleaned in the last few years of the grime and soot which thickly encrusted it.

Despite its moderate dimensions the interior gives an impression of peculiar spaciousness, enhanced by the consistent excellence of its proportions, the beauty of its lighting, and the uninterrupted line of the vault through both nave and choir. The piers, with their unusual stone seating round the bases, are built of massive blocks of unpolished Purbeck marble, sharply and exquisitely moulded into a multiplicity of shafts (11), their bluish grey contrasting with the yellow sandstone of the arcade. The low band of the triforium stage consists of a blind arcade of small trefoil-headed arches, four to a bay and surmounted by an elegant pierced parapet made up of a double row of quatrefoils. Above this rise the spacious windows of the clerestory, and over all the splendid vault springs from shafts which descend low towards the moulded capitals of the piers and terminate in tapering corbels of massed foliage, with occasional figures, which include some of the cathedral's finest carving. The central and lateral ridge lines have a series of carved bosses, the best of which are in the choir, with such subjects as the Crucifixion and the murder of Becket alternating with the foliations beloved of the Exeter craftsmen.

The presbytery and choir (41) form the noblest part of the building, dating from the close of the thirteenth century and the first few years of the fourteenth, a period when the style, unshackled from precedent, blossomed into a short spring of loveliness that was soon again to lose its freshness in a new subjection; the Perpendicular east window, however, is an insertion of

Ely: *the exterior of the Octagon and its lantern*

38 Ely: the Octagon, looking across the transepts.
Octagon designed by 'Master John', probably
John of Ramsey, 1322–46; timber vaults and
lantern by William Hurley, 1328–40

39   *Exeter: the west front, 1346–75, in part designed by William Joy*

40   *Exeter: the east end, c. 1275–1308, from the south*

the late fourteenth century. The proportions, mouldings, and carvings are as nearly perfect as is possible to the human mind, the only comparable work of the same period being in the chapter-house at Southwell. The preservation of most of the fabric rolls allows us to follow the construction very closely at many points and learn something of the men responsible for the achievement. The carver of all this beauty of corbel and boss was William of Montacute in Somerset; his portrait can be seen under the figure of St Catherine in one of the corbels. The choir fortunately retains some of its original furniture, including the canopied bishop's throne, 57 feet high and incorporating some of the finest wood carving in England; together with the stalls at Winchester and Lancaster and the sedilia at Beverley it largely forms our criterion of fourteenth-century carpentry. Up to the close of this period the carpenter followed the mason's ideals—the work, when coloured and gilt, might easily be taken for stone. This throne may have been designed by Master Thomas de Winton who came to Exeter in this connection in 1313, being paid 3s. a week and 5s. for his journey home. The head carpenter, Robert of Galmpton, was paid 2s. 6d. a week, and the head carver Walter of Membury 2s. 9d., both of these being Devon men. The great reredos, since destroyed, with its fifty statues and silver dorsal, the tall sedilia and the *pulpitum*, followed shortly after the throne. The last named is only partly preserved, the solid wall on the choir side having been broken through, but Scott, to his credit, managed to save the whole from demolition. The upper gallery of panels originally contained sculpture (the roll for 1322–1323 mentions '45 images for 11 panels, with a Doom'), and the present paintings are of the Stuart period. Under the Commonwealth a wall was erected at the crossing, dividing the cathedral into two preaching churches, 'East' and 'West Peter's', for the use of different Puritan sects. The credit for its removal belongs to Bishop Seth Ward, of happy memory, who after the Restoration spent some £25,000 on necessary repairs and renovations.

The building of the nave was interrupted by the Black Death, and when the pestilence had abated no glaziers could be found, so that the windows had temporarily to be made up with wattle and daub. The piers were worked at the Purbeck quarries by the Canons, father and son, and shipped from Dorset to Topsham, the port of Exeter. The beautiful minstrels' gallery in the north triforium was built for the Palm Sunday services, and is faced with niches containing angels playing musical instruments. The west window incorporates in its head a splendid circle filled with tracery; its eighteenth-century heraldic glass by Peckett of York was removed in 1904, but some survives in the deanery and in the portion of the cloisters reconstructed by Pearson. The exquisite Renaissance marble font was set up in 1684. In the transepts the corbelled galleries were added by Quivil to complete a continuous triforium passage round the building; in the northern transept is Exeter's well known astronomical clock.

Throughout the cathedral the chapels and chantries form a fascinating series, with their beautiful late Gothic screens of wood and stone; some of their woodwork has now been amazingly reconstructed after being shattered when the cathedral was bombed in 1942. The tombs and monuments are of particular note, including the effigies of various bishops from Bartholomew, who died in 1184, to Cotton whose death was in 1621. The coloured figure of Bishop Bronescombe (d. 1280) is of special beauty and splendour. So too is that of Bishop Stafford (d. 1419), and his relative Canon Langton is commemorated by a good kneeling brass. Sometimes, as with the tombs of Bronescombe and Stafford under their canopies added late in the fifteenth century (13), these tombs are matched, with typical Exeter symmetry, across the church; the same correspondence of plan, though not in detail, is seen in the rich sixteenth-century chantry chapels of Bishop Oldham and Sir John Speke. A curious little chapel built between the western image screen and the west wall of the nave once contained the tomb of Bishop Grandisson. The Elizabethan and Jacobean monuments are of considerable variety and include one to Sir John Gilbert (d. 1596), who was Raleigh's half-brother. The half-length figure of Canon Cotton (d. 1675) is of special beauty among the later memorials, and the modern tablets in the nave include one to R. D. Blackmore, the author of *Lorna Doone*.

The rectangular chapter-house which adjoins the south tower was built in the thirteenth century and given a new upper stage in the fifteenth century when the large windows were put in. The Bishop's Palace, whose garden envelops the cathedral's east end, contains a thirteenth-century chapel 'improved' by Butterfield.

The cathedral was directly hit in the 'Baedeker' raids which much damaged the city in 1942. Part of the south choir aisle, and the chapel of St James adjoining it, were brought down, but the damage has now been made good in a replica of the old work.

GLOUCESTER

The Cathedral Church of the Holy and Indivisible Trinity, formerly the Abbey of St Peter

The first religious house of St Peter at Gloucester was founded in 681 by Osric, who was the sub-king of the Hwiccas (who dwelt in what later became Gloucestershire and Worcestershire), and a viceroy of King Ethelred of Mercia; his sister Kyneburga was appointed abbess of a dual foundation of monks and nuns. In the ninth century the church was rebuilt in stone, and secular priests replaced the religious. But in 1022 Canute, to quote Leland, 'for ill lyvinge expellyd secular clerks, and by the counsell of Wolstane, Bysschope of Wurcester,* bringethe in monkes'. These monks were Benedictines, and their unpopularity was partly justified by the laxity of their morals and discipline. In 1058, however, the monastery was taken in hand by Aldred, Bishop of Worcester, who rebuilt the church on a larger scale. In 1072, on the death of the Saxon abbot, a Norman monk named Serlo was appointed in his place; he found the establishment shrunk to two monks and eight novices. Serlo, with great energy and ability, brought new life to a declining foundation and soon so increased the number of monks that rebuilding was again thought necessary. The present church, commencing with its early Norman crypt, was begun in 1089 and was consecrated in 1100 by a concourse of bishops.

It is uncertain how much of the Norman abbey church was complete at the time of the consecration, but the nave was certainly finished several years later. For two more centuries the fabric rolls show little more than a catalogue of comparatively minor alterations and additions. It was after the accession of Abbot Wigmore (1329–1337) that the second important phase began in the evolution of the building as we know it today. The murder of the deposed King Edward II at Berkeley Castle in 1327 transformed, in popular imagination, a weak neurotic king into the semblance of a saint and martyr. His body had been refused burial by the abbots of Bristol, Kingswood, and Malmesbury, but Abbot Thokey of Gloucester, with commendable loyalty to a sovereign he had more than once entertained, 'fetched him from Berkeley Castle in his own chariot, sumptuously adorned

---

* Not to be confused with the second, and canonised, Wulstan, who ruled the Worcester diocese (in which most of Gloucestershire then lay) from 1062 to 1095.

and painted with the arms of our monastery, and brought him to Gloucester, where all the convent received him honourably in their solemn robes, with a procession of the whole city, and buried him in our church, in the north aisle, hard by the high altar'. King Edward III's desire for the worthy commemoration of his father combined with the offerings of visitors to urge forward the creation of what would, in effect, be a specially glorious memorial chapel to house the King's tomb which was piously erected by his son and successor. Abbot Wigmore was a man of taste and discrimination, and he may well have been aided by the eminent Court mason William Ramsey in his scheme for a great cage of decorative panelling, which would wholly transform the appearance of a choir at the same time made more lofty and splendid. The soft, white local stone was used, not only to create what was one of the most lovely and original works of later English Gothic, but to make a major contribution to an architectural revolution whose influence persisted for two hundred years. Abbot Morewent (1421–1437) made a start on the rebuilding of the nave, and Abbot Seabroke (1450–1457) began the great central tower. Before it was finished, a start was made on the present Lady Chapel which replaced a demolished thirteenth-century building. The nineteenth century saw an irritating but restricted restoration by Scott, at whose hands a number of the delightful Renaissance fittings shown by Britton vanished.

The cathedral now stands pleasantly in a Close of old houses. From the inner city the only really good view is the vista from Westgate Street, which was brilliantly opened up by various new building developments completed in 1959, but the best prospects are to be had from the low water-meadows by the Severn, whence the tall central tower and clerestory appear splendidly conspicuous above a grouping of roofs. Similarly, at close range (1) it is the richly panelled and tabernacled Perpendicular tower, 225 feet high, which largely dominates the composition, rising in tiers of canopies to a crowning storey of open stonework, with four lofty pinnacles connected by a pierced parapet. The cathedral's principal elements—nave, choir, and Lady Chapel —form an uneven roofline of three levels. Save for the projecting porch of the fifteenth century, and for its south aisle as rebuilt by Abbot Thokey with large Decorated windows and 'ballflower' ornament, the exterior of the nave is fairly plain in elevation. Despite the insertion of fourteenth-century windows, whose tracery is a cross between Decorated and Perpendicular, the transepts, with their arcaded turrets, remain largely Norman in their fabric, as also are the choir aisles, with their projecting apsidal chapels; here

41   *Exeter: the choir, 1288–1308, looking to the east window, 1390–91. Choir designed by Master Roger; east window by Robert Lesyngham. Bishop's Throne, c. 1316, Robert of Galmpton carpenter*

42 Gloucester: the south walk of the cloisters, 1381–1412, possibly by Robert Lesyngham

43   Gloucester: Norman piers in the nave, c. 1100–60. Vault, 1242–45, possibly by John of Gloucester

44 Gloucester: the choir, 1337–50, probably designed by William Ramsey; stalls of fourteenth century

45 Gloucester: the Lady Chapel, c. 1470, looking west to the gallery–bridge. Possibly designed by John Hobbs

also, however, there are windows of mainly Decorated type inserted into the thickness of the earlier walls. Above rise the tall windows of the early Perpendicular clerestory, surmounted by a pierced parapet, which curves upwards at the east end, above the ogee curve of the east window's hood-mould, to a lofty open work gable flanked by most graceful turrets. Complete in itself, the great Lady Chapel stands a little apart from the east end of the main church, being connected to the cathedral by an ambulatory bridge. It is most beautiful and stately in its Perpendicular fenestration, which is typical also of the college chapels of its period (*c.* 1470).

The seven Norman bays of the nave (*43*) are fine and massive work, of the same west-country type as at Tewkesbury though more ornate and probably a few years later. They consist of an arcade of cylindrical piers, 30 feet high to the plainly moulded capitals; they are narrowly spaced and carry rather meagre round-headed arches, well and plainly moulded and with an order of chevron ornament. The triforium is rather insignificant, consisting of a coupled arcade of four small arches to each bay, flanked on each side by the clustered Purbeck shafts of the thirteenth-century vault, which was somewhat clumsily built by the monks' own hands; its low springing resulted in a bad misfit which divided the clerestory windows into isolated compartments, improving neither the lighting nor the symmetry. The north aisle has a plain, Norman ribbed vault, but in the south aisle the vault was reconstructed early in the fourteenth century. The two western bays, and the west front, were rebuilt under Abbot Morewent about 1430, following on the demolition of the Norman west towers, whose walls in part survive and whose dimensions account for the fact that the western of the two fifteenth-century bays is twice as long as the other. The vaulting here is of a complex ribbed pattern, with some fine carved bosses. An eighteenth-century scheme to transform the nave's appearance by fluting the Norman piers, originating with no less an architect than William Kent (who also inserted a Georgian Gothic screen which has now disappeared), was happily thwarted. It is, however, pleasant to find that some oak fittings of about 1680 have survived, contrasting with the florid Victorian outburst of Clayton and Bell in the windows.

East of the nave aisles, the delicate transformation started under Abbot Wigmore appears in utter contrast to the solidity of the nave. The conception lying behind this transformation of Gloucester's choir (*44*) and transepts has, at least, in part been traced to the Severn valley school of masons, who in the earlier years of the fourteenth century produced such

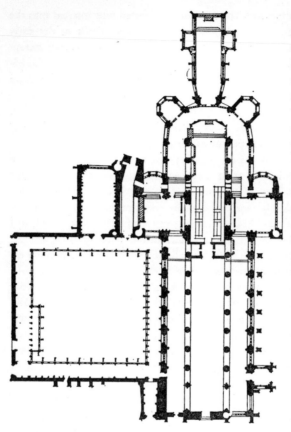

exciting structural novelties as the open-arch vaulting in Bristol Cathedral and the great trio of inverted arches which encloses the crossing at Wells. In the eastern limb at Gloucester the experiment was crystallised in a new style of surface decoration, a style of skeleton, cagelike panelling and vast transomed windows of many lights, with slender moulded mullions carried vertically to the heads of those windows and leading the eye towards the magnificent vault. The casing of the inner side of the Romanesque work was effected with a dexterous economy both of materials and labour, and as a scheme of decoration it was soon imitated at Glastonbury, but remained unsurpassed in the two centuries' achievement of the Perpendicular style which it so largely engendered.

The transepts were included in the reconditioning, and the southern one was in fact done earlier than the presbytery. Large new windows were inserted in their ends, and the transepts themselves were roofed with complex lierne vaults, that in the south transept being skilfully put together without bosses. In the north transept, beneath a richly bossed vault, the thirteenth-century 'reliquary', with Purbeck shafting and plate tracery, strikes a somewhat discordant note. A curious effect results from the appearance in the

south transept of the fifteenth-century internal flying buttresses, or massive
stone struts, which support the tower, and at the crossing the transept arches
are spanned by 'flying arches' of light masonry which seem, from a heraldic
corbel, to date from before 1340. The view up the choir is of unforgettable
beauty. In its delicate yet insistent verticality, and in its spaciousness and
brilliant lighting, the design unmistakably foreshadows the great Perpendicular royal or college chapels, with its clerestory range in effect an
immense single lantern. It ends in an expanse of glass which fills the entire
east end of the building. This vast window is canted outward in three planes
to give a greater area and stronger wind resistance, and contains most of its
original glass, which commemorates the men of Gloucestershire who fought
at Crécy. Crowning all is the lierne vault, a little tedious in its complexity
but containing a profusion of sculptured bosses and, over the sanctuary, an
enchanting group of carved angels playing on instruments. The canopied
stalls, though much restored, are a remarkable achievement of the
mid-fourteenth century, with niche-like and slightly protruding canopies and a wealth of misericords. The tomb of Edward II remains
under the north arcade, its profuse canopy work contrasting with the
simple dignity of its alabaster effigy, one of the earliest carved examples
of that material in England. It is curious to compare this work with
the stiff, sword-drawing effigy of the Conqueror's eldest son Robert of
Normandy, who died in captivity in 1134 and was buried here at
Gloucester. The figure is of the thirteenth century and retains traces of its
colouring.

In the choir's reconstruction the Norman aisles were left intact, being
roofed with transverse arches and heavy groined vaults and forming a curved
ambulatory round the presbytery. The triforium passage forms a second
storey, with the broad arches of its arcade now delicately patterned by the
shafts and transoms of the Perpendicular inner casing. It is roofed by a plain
demi berceau, or half-barrel vault, and completing the connection around the
east end is a little passage built out from the main fabric and called the
'whispering gallery' from its acoustic properties. It passes over the vestibule
of the Lady Chapel (45), and from this virtual bridge a view is obtained
of the interior of that lovely building, conceived on similar lines to the choir
though finished about 150 years later. To all intents and purposes it is walled
with mullions and glass. Its east window is of nine lights, and facing it at
the west end the vaulted vestibule is surmounted by a magnificent nine-light
screen of Perpendicular tracery. Over all is an elaborate lierne vault, and the

two miniature transepts contain little chapels with open musicians' galleries in their upper storeys.

Apart from its royal tombs the cathedral has a posthumous monument of Osric (not erected till the early years of the sixteenth century), and several monuments to pre-Reformation abbots and to bishops—Pope's associate Warburton among them—who have held the see since it was established by Henry VIII in 1541. Other post-Reformation monuments well exemplify the truth that a cathedral can become a veritable pantheon of local and county worthies. Many of these are by the Gloucester firms of Bryan, Ricketts, or Wood, while Flaxman's relief to Mrs Sarah Morley, who died at sea in 1784, is one of his more notable compositions. More important still are the superb marble recumbent effigies of Alderman Abraham Blackleech (d. 1639) and his wife, and Thomas Green of Camberwell's canopied standing figure of Judge Powell (d. 1723), a monument which proves England not to have been lacking in its minor masterpieces of Baroque art.

The cloisters (42) are the finest in England, their glory being the fan-vault, continuous round all sides and possibly the first such vault to be constructed. The *scriptorium* in the south alleyway is almost as it was left by the monks, with twenty small compartments, or carrels, for the desks of the writers. In the north walk, near the site of the destroyed refectory, is the most complete surviving *lavatorium* for the monks' ablutions, preserving its stone towel cupboard. On the east side is the rectangular Norman chapter-house, roofed with a pointed barrel-vault and lit by a large Perpendicular window at the east end. Between this and the north transept is the vaulted Norman slype which forms the undercroft of a later library. A second passage at the north-east corner leads to the ruined arcade of the infirmary, and a miniature cloister here encloses what was probably the 'farmery garth', or herb garden for medicinal supplies. On the cloister's western side the Old Deanery (now Church House) was once the prior's, and earlier the abbot's, house. It is a most interesting blend of Norman and later architecture, and some fine Jacobean panelling was put in by the future Archbishop Laud when he was Dean of Gloucester from 1616 to 1621.

HEREFORD

The Cathedral Church of St Mary and St Ethelbert

This moderate-sized cathedral stands pleasantly amid its lawns in a busy county town, and its tower forms the central feature in some attractive views from over the Wye. The bishopric was founded late in the seventh century when the much larger Midland diocese of Lichfield was split up. Another Saxon church was raised about 825 above the tomb of St Ethelbert, the King of East Anglia who was said to have been put to death in 792 by the great Offa of Mercia. The Saxon cathedral was destroyed in a Welsh raid a few years before the Norman Conquest, and nothing of it now remains. It was replaced, towards the end of the eleventh century and in the first decades of the twelfth, by a Romanesque cathedral started by Robert de Losinga. The eastern wall of the south transept, an interesting work of early Norman type with a most careful arrangement of three-tiered arcading on its blank east wall which has the vaulted treasury behind it, is probably the oldest part of the existing building. The reconstructed choir, and the heavily scraped and restored nave arcades are likely to date from about 1110–1145. More puzzling is the fine Transitional work in the retrochoir, but the Early English Lady Chapel, which lies east of it, was completed by about 1225. About forty years later the north transept was rebuilt, to a striking design, under Bishop Aquablanca whose tomb, with its highly important early canopy in the wiry Geometrical style, lies in it. Thomas de Cantilupe, who became Bishop of Hereford in 1275, was one of the most notable prelates of the thirteenth century; he was a man of great sanctity and was canonised after his death in Italy in 1282. His bones were brought back to Hereford by Richard Swinfield his chaplain, and a shrine was duly erected over them. Swinfield succeeded Cantilupe as bishop and made numerous additions to the cathedral, as also did Adam of Orleton, another famous politician-bishop who rebuilt the central tower about 1316–1320; it long had a timber spire which has now disappeared. A tower was also built over the west end in the fourteenth century, but this collapsed in 1786. The architect Wyatt then did important alterations and repairs, and since his time there have been three major restorations, aesthetically deplorable but including the remarkable nineteenth-century engineering feat which almost certainly saved the central tower.

This sturdy tower (47), with its pinnacles modern and with its worn

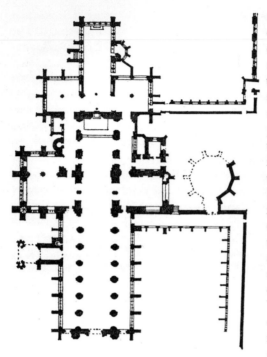

sandstone encrusted with crumbling 'ballflower' ornament, is easily the most impressive feature of the exterior. The two-storeyed north porch is a most distinguished Perpendicular addition to the earlier porch behind it. A chapel is above this porch, and the whole building was completed in 1518 or 1519. The collapse of the western tower opened the way for a series of drastic reconstructions over a period of more than a century. Wyatt's somewhat weakly designed west front was replaced in the early years of this century by a ponderously ornate one by J. Oldrid Scott. At the east end, the Lady Chapel, heavily restored in the nineteenth century by Cottingham, has something of the appearance of a recent school chapel. Inside the cathedral the most continuous piece of old work is in the Norman nave arcades (49), with their cylindrical piers, capitals carved with close interlacements, and moulded arches. The triforium and clerestory represent a Gothic design by Wyatt (who shortened the nave by one bay), and his vault is a good version of a fourteenth-century one, in painted wood with fine bosses.

It is hard to write with enough detestation about the tortured 'art metalwork' screen installed by Sir Gilbert Scott. It contains 11,200 lb. of iron, 5,000 lb. of copper and brass, 50,000 pieces of mosaic and 300 cut stones. Slightly ravaged by oxidisation and by the wear and tear of nearly a century, it was much admired by the Victorians when it was new, and stands as a melancholy commentary on the transience of even the most eminent taste.

The transepts show the greatest architectural contrasts in Hereford cathedral's fabric. The southern one, as we have seen, is in the main a structure of the Norman period, perhaps as early as the 1090s. The northern one (50) was rebuilt, about 1260, to a remarkable Geometrical design. The main arches in its arcade are almost triangular, the heads of the triforium arches each have three pierced quatrefoils, and the spandrels have rich diapering. The exceedingly tall and slender windows with their Geometrical tracery are both rare and delightful, being of a type very seldom found in England. The pedestal of St Thomas Cantilupe's shrine has been moved to this transept; it is arcaded with Purbeck shafting and in its lower panels has fifteen figures of Knights Templar, members of an Order of which the canonised bishop was Provincial Grand Master.

The choir, with its somewhat gloomy interior, is of a Norman design which recalls that of the nave arcades, though with compound piers, a massive triforium, and a fine Early English vaulted clerestory. It terminates eastward in a much-restored Norman arch (once leading into the apse) through which one can see the central vaulting pier of the Lady Chapel vestibule. The upper spandrel of this pier is now loaded with indifferent Victorian sculpture, replacing, as a background to the high altar, Bishop Bisse's great classical reredos of the early eighteenth century which was removed in 1841. The bishop's throne and the choir stalls are very fine original woodwork of the fourteenth century.

The small eastern transepts, in the Decorated style though of separate dates, form a single composition with the retrochoir. The Lady Chapel, low, but quite spacious, and built over an important thirteenth-century vaulted crypt, is of an Early English design whose most distinctive feature is the deep recessing of its shafted lancets. Off the south side one enters the two-storeyed Perpendicular chantry of Bishop Audley (1492–1502) who built another chantry at Salisbury, to which bishopric he was transferred. Here at Hereford his chapel is half-octagonal in shape, and is beautifully panelled and fan-vaulted.

Hereford Cathedral is notably rich in its mediaeval monuments, commemorating both bishops and some of the local aristocracy. It also has more surviving brasses than any other cathedral in England; of these the best is the fine canopied one of Bishop Trilleck who died in 1360. The post-Reformation monuments are not of much note, though Roubiliac's bust of James Thomas (d. 1757) is worth seeing. Out in the precincts, only two walks remain of the fifteenth-century cloisters, and the demolition of the two-storeyed Romanesque Bishop's Chapel, which took place in the Georgian period, was an irreparable loss. The unobtrusive Vicars' Cloister, with its quaintly carved roof timbers, leads to the delightful quadrangle of the College of the Vicars Choral. The chained library (*48*), now replaced over the eastern aisle of the north transept, should certainly be visited. An even greater treasure, and the outstanding rarity of Hereford, is the famous *Mappa Mundi*, probably dating from about 1290 and giving us a priceless insight into mediaeval ideas on cosmography and mapmaking.

LICHFIELD
The Cathedral Church of St Mary

What must once have been among the loveliest of the smaller cathedrals stands on rising ground on the edge of a quiet Midland city. Its immediate surroundings are very beautiful, its trio of spires rising in graceful precision above an old mill pool on the southern side. It is built of an attractive reddish sandstone, but at close range the effect is disappointing, for the fabric has suffered so drastically from destroyers, restorers, and atmospheric pollution that its present appearance is largely that of an elaborate production of last century. The west front (*46*) is the dominant external feature; from a distance its appearance can have changed little since early in the fourteenth century, though a modern Geometrical west window was allowed to replace the interesting flamboyant Gothic stonework inserted after the ravages of the Civil War. Except for the flanking turrets it is a flat façade designed purely for surface treatment, consisting of two spire-capped towers with a steeply gabled nave between them. The scheme of decoration, largely destroyed in the seventeenth and eighteenth centuries, was in three stages, with close-set ranges of canopied statues now replaced by Victorian banalities. The great west door is largely a modern reconstruction of a strikingly original and beautiful design, and the portals of the transepts are of a somewhat similar though earlier type, having double apertures within containing arches of many orders of carved mouldings; that on the north, through which the bishop entered from his Palace, is the more elaborate. These also, however, have been to a large extent rebuilt, with modern statues. The central tower carries the tallest of Lichfield's three spires, rebuilt after its destruction in the Civil War and a good version of the fourteenth-century work, with its windows affording a clear view through the structure, which went before it.

46   Lichfield from the north-west. Lower part of west front, c. 1280-93, probably by Thomas Wallace;
upper part, 1294-1327; spires, probably c. 1385, by Gilbert Mason

47 *Hereford from the north-west, show-ing the tower, c. 1325, the north transept, c. 1250–68, and Bishop Booth's porch, c. 1520–30. West front by J. Oldrid Scott, 1908*

48 *Hereford: the chained library*

49 Hereford: the Norman piers of the nave, c. 1100–45; triforium and vault by Wyatt after 1786

50 Hereford: the Geometrical design of the north transept, c. 1250–68

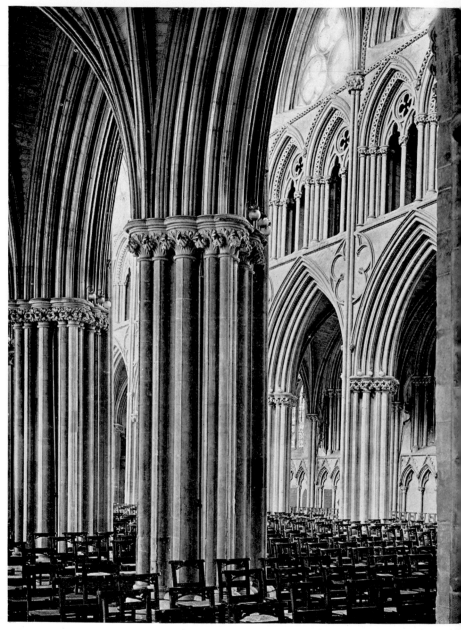

51   Lichfield: the nave, 1250–80, from the south aisle. Possibly designed by William Fitzthomas

St Chad, who died in 672 and was the greatest of Mercia's missionary bishops, was the original patron of the cathedral which was largely rebuilt from offerings at his shrine. Nothing is known of the history or architecture of the successive Saxon churches, but it is certain that a new and much larger building, with an apsidal eastern limb, was begun under Robert de Lymesey, the first Norman bishop. This was towards the close of the eleventh century, at a time when the fortunes of the large diocese were decidedly chequered. For a few years the bishopric was centred at Chester, and then in the monastic cathedral at Coventry. Eventually, however, like the Somerset bishopric with its two cathedrals, the see settled down as that of Coventry and Lichfield, a monastic chapter being in the earlier, and now obliterated, Coventry Cathedral, and secular canons at Lichfield. The destruction of documents and archives in the Civil War has left the fabric's early history somewhat nebulous, but there is little doubt that work on the present cathedral started with the building of the three western bays of the choir about 1195; this section of the eastern limb was ultimately remodelled and assimilated to later work. The development of the cathedral in its present form occupied about 150 years, the artistic culmination of the work being the building of the Lady Chapel during the splendid episcopate (1296–1321) of Walter Langton who was a friend of Edward I and Lord Treasurer of England; at the same time he erected a shrine to St Chad at the then enormous cost of £2,000. Langton was also responsible for the fortification of the Close with an embattled wall which remained till the Civil War, when in 1643 the precincts were occupied by Royalists against a besieging force led by the fanatical Lord Brooke, who was 'so great a zealot against the established discipline of the Church, that no less than the utter extirpation of episcopacy, and abolishing all decent order in the service of God, would satisfy him; to which end he became the leader of all the power he could raise for the destruction of the cathedral of Coventry and Litchfield'. Brooke, while planting his cannon against the south-east gate of the Close, was shot dead by a deaf-mute named Dyott from the parapet of the main steeple. The Close was then for three days subjected to a gruelling bombardment which wrought terrible havoc on the cathedral; this was followed after its surrender by wholesale destruction in its interior by Roundhead soldiery. It was recorded that at the Restoration the vestry was the only part left with a roof where it was possible to conduct service. It is to the credit of the Restoration Chapter and to the first bishop of the new régime, the admirable Hackett (1662–1670), that immense energy and vast sums were devoted to

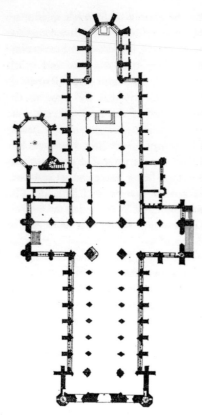

the restoration of the battered church to something approaching its ancient dignity. Structural repairs apart, new stalls and a throne, of more Renaissance character than those set up by Cosin at Durham, were placed in the choir. Of these the throne, of an ornately Renaissance design, survives in the Consistory Court, having been replaced in the choir by a neo-Gothic confection carved by an uncle of 'George Eliot'. Late in the eighteenth century some restoration and re-arrangement was done at Lichfield by Wyatt, who was himself a Staffordshire man.

Spick and span from the hands of its refurbishers, the interior has been described by Professor Prior as 'offensive to taste for the same reason that china reproductions of the Venus of Milo or the oleographs of the Sistine Madonna are offensive'. Britton's plates of 1822 show a work of considerable decorative magnificence sadly damaged and decayed, but the restorers, essential as was some of their work, are to be blamed for choosing to reconstruct rather than repair, causing inevitable and evident falsification; it is, however, to their credit that they spared many (but not all) of the Perpendicular windows inserted in the fifteenth century to increase the light available in the choir and transepts.

The nave (51) is built to a rich design of about 1250–1280; it consists of a closely spaced arcade, with bold multiple mouldings, also with well carved foliate capitals, and with graceful cinquefoils each one of which runs into two of the spandrels and is divided down the middle by a vaulting shaft descending all the way to the floor. The arcade is surmounted by a tall, arcaded triforium of some elaboration, and the nave's lack of height is emphasised by the unusual shape of the Geometrical clerestory windows which are triangular with curved sides. The early Gothic crossing arches, on lofty clustered piers, are particularly fine, and the Early English transepts (with no triforium stage, many Perpendicular windows and a ribbed vault added in the fourteenth century) end, in the northern one, with a group of five modern lancets, and, in the southern, with a large nine-light Perpendicular window and heavy supporting buttresses added by Wyatt. In the choir, we have seen how the three western bays were early Gothic work of about 1195. But with the addition of the five remaining bays of the structural choir, the foliage of their capitals betokening their fourteenth-century date, the whole eastern limb was remodelled and the present clerestory, with its charming parapet of cusped triangles, was added. So too was the entire choir vault, and the resulting effect of 'unification' may be compared with what was later done at Wells. The choir's design dispenses with a triforium, but below each of the tall clerestory windows of Perpendicular design a section of cusped panelling, with an embattled parapet above, takes a triforium's place. The upper windows, except in the bay before the Lady Chapel, are lined on the splays with a beautiful patterned relief of quatrefoils. The hideous screen, the reredos, and most of the other fittings were put in by Scott, who was also responsible for the listless statuary over his angel corbels. The beautiful sedilia are made up of fragments of the old reredos.

The Lady Chapel, of the same internal height as the choir, forms an apsidal termination to the east end and is easily the finest part of the building with its steep-pitched vault and tall, narrow six- or three-light windows with trefoils in their heads. Seven of these are filled with superb glass, of dates ranging from 1532 to 1538, which was brought early last century from the Cistercian abbey of Herckenrode in Flanders. Other glass of interest in the cathedral was made in 1811 by the Shrewsbury glazier John Betton. There are also some fine late Victorian windows by Kempe. The chapter-house, an elongated octagon, is entered through a charming vestibule from the north choir aisle. It was built about 1240–1250, is vaulted from a central pier with a richly foliated capital, and is lined continuously with trefoiled wall arcading. Its upper storey is used as a library and contains some rare mediaeval manuscripts. Other notable buildings in the precincts are the delightful Renaissance Palace, which is dated 1687, and Vicars' Close, a mediaeval courtyard whose construction is largely in picturesque half-timbering.

Except for two fine thirteenth-century bishops' effigies in dark marble, nearly all the cathedral's mediaeval memorials were destroyed in the Civil

War. Bishop Hackett's marble tomb, with its mitred and vested effigy, is among the most notable of later dates, while Chantrey is very well represented by his kneeling statue of Bishop Ryder, put up in 1841, and by his masterpiece, dated 1817, of the two sleeping Robinson children. Other memorials in the cathedral are peculiarly rich in their literary associations. The busts of the local celebrity Dr Johnson, and of David Garrick, were set up in 1793 and are inaccurate likenesses. The excellent Ionic mural to Dean Addison (d. 1703) was erected by his literary son in 1719, which was the year of Joseph Addison's own death. Another mural posthumously commemorates Lady Mary Wortley Montagu who was born at Lichfield; its inscription mainly recalls her as a pioneer of vaccination.

LINCOLN
The Cathedral Church of St Mary

The abrupt hill on which Lincoln Minster stands has been the site of a settlement since prehistoric times. On it the Romans built a city within massive quadrangular walls, fragments of which survive, and it is some gauge of its importance that it marked the intersection point of no less than five imperial roads, including the Fosse Way and Ermine Street. As a Saxon town it is said to have been converted to Christianity by Paulinus, the indomitable missionary bishop of York, about 628, and a stone church was built on the site of the present St Paul's in Bailgate. The original seat of the diocese, however, was the village of Stow about eleven miles north-west of Lincoln. This has been identified as the ancient Sidnaceaster, and the church built there contained the bishop's stool of the new diocese of Lindsey, maintaining its line of bishops for over 200 years. About 870 the church at Stow was burnt by the Norsemen, and Lincoln itself fell into the hands of the invaders, and became the chief of the 'Five Boroughs' of the Danish confederation. During the tenth century the seat of the bishopric was removed for safety to Dorchester-on-Thames, in a remote corner of the diocese, and here it remained till after the Norman Conquest. William's new bishop, Remigius of Fécamp, transferred it finally to Lincoln where the building of a new castle and cathedral was soon started.

Remigius's church was some twenty years in building—a grim, fortress-like structure, part of whose fabric is included in the present west front. About 1141 the burning of the roof provided an incentive for the third bishop of the new line, Alexander the Magnificent, an ambitious and energetic builder, virtually to reconstruct the cathedral. The Norman west doorways date from this period. So too do the lower stages of the two western towers, and the flanking gables of those towers gave to the west end the appearance, on an embryonic scale, of a Rhineland Romanesque *westwerk*. During the reign of Stephen the building was seized by the king and for a time garrisoned as a fortress; its fabric must have suffered some damage during these stormy years when Lincoln Castle, continually attacked and be-sieged, was a formidable stronghold of the 'Empress' Matilda's faction. In 1185 some kind of earthquake, severe enough to be felt throughout England, occurred at Lincoln. The Minster was 'cleft from top to bottom', and the damage seems to have been beyond repair. Next year a new bishop was appointed to the diocese, the famous St Hugh of Lincoln. Under his direction the building of a new cathedral on revolutionary lines was begun in 1192. 'What Diocletian did at Spalato for the round arch', wrote Freeman, 'St. Hugh did at Lincoln for the pointed arch'. The great bishop died in 1200, but the work he had begun, though much damaged by the collapse of the central tower, was slowly brought to maturity throughout the thirteenth century, largely under the supervision of another famous builder, Bishop Robert Grosseteste (1235–1253). Operations culminated about 1280 in the completion of the Angel Choir, 'one of the loveliest of human works', designed as a resting place for the relics of the canonised Bishop Hugh. Its splendid consecration was attended by Edward I and Queen Eleanor, and by a great assembly of nobles, knights, and bishops.

Lincoln still has much magnificence, a magnificence that begins with its situation. Its towered mass occupies the entire crown of the hill and soars easily above the roofs of the old streets which twist and climb below it; they in their turn are placed high above the smoke and noise of the modern town. From the level fen country that spreads eastward the profile of the great cathedral, reared on its hill, is a striking and conspicuous landmark for many miles.

Except for its three towers(53), and the Norman nucleus of its western structure, the Minster forms a splendid epitome of thirteenth-century building in England. Of its many façades the most ambitious is the screen wall of the west front(54) in which ranges of Early English arcading, extending some 175 feet from north to south, are broken by three tremendous

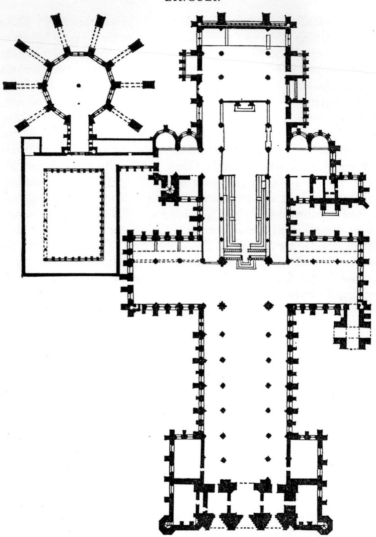

shadowed cavities which rise over the late Norman doors and are flanked by large recessed niches of the earlier Romanesque work. The section of plain wall in which these features are set formed part of Remigius's original church, and the panels of late Romanesque figure carving contrast curiously with the uncomfortably seated late fourteenth-century figures of kings which are ranged between the central doorway and the early Perpendicular west window. It is impossible here to analyse in any detail the complex evolution of this remarkable composition; but whatever its merits or demerits, the Early English extensions of it are unrelated to the design of the cathedral as a whole, and remain, as intended, purely a screen above which the twin towers, with their late Norman lower structure, Romanesque arcading, and early Perpendicular upper portions, rise a trifle abruptly.

With its two pairs of transepts and its clustering chapels and porches, Lincoln cathedral spreads its masonry over a vast, irregular plan, in a design which grows steadily in elaboration as it continues eastward. The eastern limb itself forms perhaps the richest architectural expression of its period (1256–1280) in England, with its delicate Geometrical tracery and ranges of arcaded and panelled buttresses, ending in tall crocketed pinnacles and *gablettes*. An unusual feature is seen in the north and south doors of the Angel Choir; the latter, or Judgment Porch, is the more splendid of the two and may have been specially designed for the consecration while also, like the rich Galilee porch off the south transept, providing a splendid entrance from the Bishop's Palace. Its doorway, behind a shallow compartment of ribbed vaulting, has magnificent figure and foliate sculpture and is flanked by the two little late Perpendicular chantry chapels of Bishops Russell (1480–1494) and Longland (1521–1547); the former is now notable for its mural paintings, completed in 1958, by Duncan Grant.

On the north side of the Angel Choir is the chapter-house, with its stately radiating buttresses, adjoined by the green cloister garth; from this enclosure is obtained one of the most remarkable views of the main structure, rising in tier upon tier of masonry, bristling with pinnacles and spanned by graceful buttresses, the whole culminating in the tallest and one of the stateliest central towers in England. This, above its thirteenth-century lower stages with their rare lattice-work ornament (also seen on the tower of Newark church), is a masterpiece of the early fourteenth century, exquisite in proportion as in detail. It once carried a timber and lead spire which may have been the highest in the country, and its attractive parapet and its present pinnacles are works of the eighteenth century.

As one enters the cathedral by the main west door, one passes the bases of the western towers whose interiors were vaulted late in the fourteenth century, being adorned with panelling and arcading whose cusping has an almost Moorish silhouette and elaboration. The comparatively small, round-headed arches below those towers were set up in the 1720s, below masonry inserted to strengthen the towers themselves, to designs by James Gibbs. The Gothic arch (correctly designed in the manner of thirteenth-century work in other parts of the Minster) below which one passes into the nave is by the Cambridge Georgian architect James Essex, an important forerunner of the Gothic Revival in its more scholarly aspects. One's first impression of the interior is of spaciousness and restrained dignity, with a deft economy of execution which, compared with the heavier Norman methods, indicates a revolution in technique. If the thirteenth-century nave has one cardinal defect, it is one which characterises most of England's cathedrals of this period, namely the relative lowness of the vault; at Lincoln this is accentuated by the wide spacing of all but the two western bays which correspond to the large chapels of the aisles. Yet the nave remains a youthful, vigorous achievement in early Gothic building, and it is an experience not easily to be forgotten to stand at the west end and watch the swift retreat of the vault's perspective towards the east window (52). Another memorable experience is to stand at the crossing, beneath the lightly poised 130-foot vault of the central tower, and enjoy the vistas down the earlier thirteenth-century main transepts; these terminate northward in the great rose window called 'The Dean's Eye', with its contemporary glazing, and southward in the panelled splays and leaflike traceried delicacy of the curvilinear 'Bishop's Eye' (55), kaleidoscopically filled with fragments of old glass of various dates. Both transepts have eastern aisles, each divided into three small chapels, and the stone screen of the choir is a rich work of the early fourteenth century, flanked by thirteenth-century aisle doorways, both of them with a splendid display of sculpture in their arch-moulds and capitals.

St Hugh's choir, from 1192 onwards, was the first limb completed of the new Gothic cathedral. It consists of four aisled bays, with narrow eastern transepts each of which has a pair of apsidal eastern chapels. Though considerably altered after the fall of the central tower in 1237, the work is still marked by impressive simplicity, amounting almost to severity, in design and detail; the unaltered pillars have detached shafts and capitals still of Transitional type. The vaulting constitutes an ugly, and happily unique, experiment in asymmetrical ribbing, and a curious constructional device is the use of two superimposed ranges of Purbeck arcading to strengthen the aisle walls. The thirteenth-century architecture contrasts with the magnificence of the late fourteenth-century stallwork which forms the chief glory of St Hugh's choir. Its forest of carved canopies is only comparable in richness with the slightly later stalls at Chester, and here also are splendid

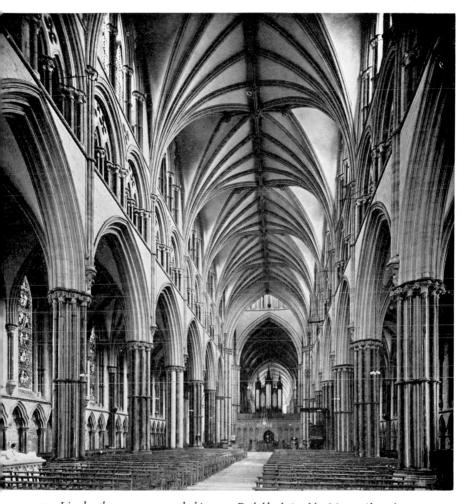

52 Lincoln: the nave, 1225–53, looking east. Probably designed by Master Alexander

53 *Lincoln from the south-west. Lower stages of west towers c. 1140–50; west front 1225–53, lower stage of central tower begun 1238, both by Master Alexander; upper stage of central tower 1306–11, by Richard of Stow; upper stages of west towers 1370–1400,*

55 Lincoln: the south transept, c. 1200–20, with the Decorated 'Bishop's Eye' window, perhaps by Master Michael

54 Lincoln: the west front, c. 1225–53, with its Norman central portion, 1074–92, and doorways, c. 1140–70

56 Lincoln: the decagonal chapter-house, c. 1220–35. Probably designed by Master Alexander

poupée heads and misericords(*8*), the latter of a playfulness as charming as anything in English carving. The wooden throne, like most of the stone reredos with its panelling and central canopy, is the work of Essex and shows hardly any Renaissance touches amid the stiff, slightly angular Gothic of its main design which recalls that of the reredos designed by Essex for King's College chapel at Cambridge. Between the stalls, the brass eagle lectern of 1667 was made in London by William Burroughes who also wrought the lecterns at Wells and Canterbury; above it hangs a superb brass chandelier of 1698.

The lovely Angel Choir(*4*), which contained the feretory and shrine of St Hugh, forms the culmination of the work at Lincoln as it also forms the culmination of the English thirteenth-century style. It was built between 1256 and 1280, and its design was clearly influenced by that of the slightly earlier presbytery at Ely. It consists of five bays, ending in a large Geometrical east window of eight lights. Its chief effect is drawn from the intricate beauty of the triforium stage, a work of supreme beauty in its incisiveness of tracery and cusping. The arches spring from clustered pillars, of which some are wholly of dark marble, and which have richly carved capitals. In the spandrels are the lovely carved angels which give this part of the cathedral its name. The slender vaulting shafts rise from foliated corbels in the spandrels of the main arcade; some have grotesque carvings below the foliage, among them the well known 'Lincoln Imp'. The east windows of the aisles retain their contemporary glass. The feretory of St Hugh has vanished, but portions remain of the shrine which contained his head, and at the east end, filling either side of the last bay, are some fine but badly broken late Gothic tombs, including those of the Burghersh family. Other mediaeval memorials in the cathedral include that by the high altar to Catherine Swynford (d. 1403) the mistress and eventually the third wife of John of Gaunt. Across the sanctuary stands the fourteenth-century Easter Sepulchre, with its profuse canopy work and reliefs of sleeping Roman soldiers. A tragic sight, as one looks at the floor in many parts of the church, is provided by the vast number of despoiled matrices of what must have been a superb display of monumental brasses. Some compensation, however, comes from the fine collection of heraldic and lettered post-Reformation floor slabs, but the other monuments of the Stuart and Georgian periods are of no great account. The best is the Baroque mural to Dean Honywood who died in 1681. More notable, in the north transept, is the exquisite mahogany pulpit in Chippendale Gothic.

The large ten-sided chapter-house (56) is one of the earliest of its type in England, dating from early in the thirteenth century. Its vaulted roof, however, supported by the characteristic central pier, is somewhat later than the rest of the building, though it is interesting to note that a similar expedient was employed at Lincoln, about 1240, in the vaulting of the northern of the twin chapels which adjoin the western towers. The cloisters date from late in the thirteenth century, and were built, standing clear of the main fabric, on the north side of the church. Their north walk is occupied by the Roman Doric arcade of the library designed by Sir Christopher Wren; it was only by a narrow margin preserved from the destructive revivalism of the last century.

LONDON
The Cathedral Church of St Paul

Of Old St Paul's, with its Norman nave, Gothic choir, tall steeple, and enormous length, only the bases of some chapter-house buttresses remain. Yet the ground plan of that cathedral, as also those of the other elongated and cruciform cathedrals surviving from mediaeval England, was a strong influence on the planning of its successor; so, too, for the classical style chosen for the new building, were the work done on Old St Paul's by Inigo Jones and the plans for its continued restoration which Wren made just before it was overwhelmed by the fire of 1666.

The Great Fire, however, only hastened and completed a process of decay which had long ravaged the fabric. Affection for the ancient building, not unmixed with civic parsimony, was at first expressed in attempts to patch and recondition the ruins. Not till 1673, after an alarming collapse of masonry in the nave, did the Royal Commission which had enquired into the matter decide finally on the demolition advocated by Sir Christopher Wren, the Surveyor General of the King's Works. Wren's talents had won him easy recognition in the spheres of mathematics and astronomy, and, while his architectural experience was at first only slight and theoretical, his approach to the practice of architecture was in the same spirit of intense scientific enquiry that had won him supremacy in other fields. The destruction of much of mediaeval London gave him a stupendous opportunity to which he rose with typical vision and vigour. Though not allowed to

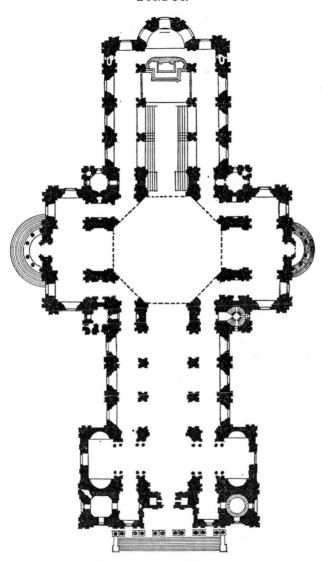

rebuild the city according to his great plan, he was allowed an almost free
hand in the rebuilding of its parish churches, whose pale stone steeples, in a
variety of slender forms, rose one after another around the growing bulk of
the great cathedral.

Before the fire Wren had put forward a scheme for altering the old fabric. The nave had already been given a classicised interior by Inigo Jones, who also added a massive Corinthian portico at the west end. Wren proposed to replace the old central tower by a lofty *rotundo* surmounted by a stone lantern. His first design for a new cathedral was for a small, simply planned rectangular building with a domed vestibule at one end. It was soon decided that something grander and more cathedralesque was needed, so Wren's next design, of which a great wooden model still exists, was of an originality very marked for any English setting. His plans were for a great centrally planned church in the form of a Greek cross, though with a short extension to the nave, and with curving corner walls to connect the cross's arms. The exterior was to be of a single storey, with a giant Corinthian order, and a vast open space was to be below the dome. The rejection of this original, intellectually daring design must have caused great grief to Wren, and was largely due to the conservatism of the clergy and to the Catholic sympathies of the Court. For these parties, being used to the elongated English cathedral with its clear division between the nave and the ritual choir, could not tolerate the idea of a plan which almost eliminated the choir and which was dominated in the middle by a central preaching space. Wren's second and very different design reverted to the conventional plan of a cruciform church with a long choir, but preserved his cherished idea of a central tholus and cupola, now due to be surmounted by a tall, rather singular steeple like those he was planning for the City churches. This design was approved by Royal Warrant, but in the long, gradual course of the cathedral's erection it underwent a mysterious, intriguing process of modification at its architect's hands. Though the cathedral as completed adhered to some of the main principles of the Warrant design, the building's exterior character was radically transformed, the 'set back' impression of its clerestory stage being changed for the continuous vertical elevation, from ground to parapet in two storeys, which one now sees. This main exterior impression is gained as a result of the screen walls which Wren built as vertical continuations of the outer walls of his aisles. At the same time the walls of his clerestory are actually in the normal position, and in the space between the two walls one finds concealed the great flying buttresses, which take the weight of the series of saucer domes covering the nave and choir. This system of roofing was a novelty in England, Wren's fondness for such domes being a feature of his mature style which was both influenced by Continental examples and by Wren's instinct of what was

57   *St Paul's: the west front, 1675–1710, by Sir Christopher Wren*

58 St Paul's: the choir,
showing the new (1958)
baldachino, and part
of Grinling Gibbons'
stalls and Tijou's iron-
work screen

59 St Paul's: the nave and
south aisle, looking west

fitted to an English environment. These qualities find their full expression
in the dome of St Paul's. On the inside this is seen as a vast airy lantern,
supported by great pendentives and by half domes at the four corners. From
without it rose, above its colonnaded drum, as a conspicuous, dignified
landmark above the comparatively low buildings of the eighteenth-century
City. These results were achieved, with great constructional ingenuity, by
building a separate, much smaller dome for interior effect and above it a
hidden brickwork cone which forms the core of the outer dome of lead-
covered timber, and at the same time carries the crowning feature of the
stone lantern which is seventy feet high. This vast, yet delicate, mass com-
poses magnificently with the two western *campanili*, themselves in their final
form works of great skill and power, and indebted for their design to the two
splendid ones by Borromini on the Roman Baroque church of St Agnese
in the Piazza Navona.

Below these western *campanili* the main façade of St Paul's was built in
two storeys with a lower and an upper portico(57); this was partly because
Wren could not obtain or transport blocks of Portland stone sufficiently
large for the giant order he favoured. The two-storeyed design continues all
round the building, and should also be studied in the apsidal east end, with
its central element raised above the later balustrade and with its crowned
cipher of Queen Anne amid floral garlands in the panel below the lower
east window. The transepts are notable for their beautiful semicircular
Corinthian porches, and in their pediments are differing sculptural designs.
One has the arms of Queen Anne, the other the Phoenix arising sym-
bolically from its ashes and also the word RESURGAM.

The stately interior of St Paul's(59), though built on a ground plan of
the proportions which had become normal in English cathedrals, is none
the less wholly unlike them in the stylistic impression which it conveys.
Not only is this due to the classical style of the arches, pillars, and pilasters,
but arises because Wren's methods of construction made it possible for the
great length of the choir and nave to be built in far fewer bays than one finds
in the average mediaeval cathedral. Above all, the dome, with its great
central space, conveys an impression of amplitude such as only the Octagon
at Ely gives us among the older cathedrals. The interior paintings, against
the wishes of Wren who would have preferred mosaics, are *grisaille* work
by Sir James Thornhill. Their effect has been vastly improved by their
recent cleaning, and they form a happy contrast to the Victorian mosaics by
Salviati and Richmond below them and in the choir.

A wealth of craftsmanship was employed on the cathedral's exterior carvings and interior decoration, all of it being brilliantly co-ordinated under Wren's supervision. The masonry was preponderantly of Portland stone. Joshua Marshall and Thomas Strong were the first master masons, the latter being succeeded by his brother Edward. A huge quantity of rubble masonry from the old building was used for filling in the ashlar-faced walls; this was an inexperienced, unscientific technique when it came to the building of the dome, and made necessary an extensive process of modern strengthening. Many carvers were employed on the external stonework, and as the pay was good the best talent was attracted. Outstanding names among these crafts-men are those of Nathaniel Rawlins, Jasper Latham, Christopher and William Kempster and, better known for their work as woodcarvers, Jonathan Maine and Grinling Gibbons. The last named was the greatest and most skilled of them all, and the brilliant elegance of his style impressed itself on the entire decorative work of the cathedral, particularly in the ornately carved choir stalls and in the rich stone swags below the choir windows. The chief statuaries were Caius Gabriel Cibber the Holsteiner, and Francis Bird who, among other works, carved the great relief of the Conversion of St Paul which fills the pediment of the west front.

The head carpenter for the constructional timber work was Richard Jennings, later succeeded by John Longland, while Charles Hopson was the most important of a group of joiners. The choir furniture, including the organ case and the stalls (with Corinthian pilasters and fine carving on their back sides as well as on their front), was carried out by Gibbons and his assistants. Maine was responsible for the woodwork of the library and for the screens of the large chapels which lead out of the nave aisles. The iron-work was mainly created by the Huguenot smith Jean Tijou, who estab-lished an English revival of this particular craft. The richly varied screens and gates of the choir, with their masterly acanthus foliage, were his great achievement, his manner being closely followed in the modern screens of the sanctuary.

The tall marble reredos by the late Victorians Bodley and Garner, over-whelming in scale and design yet not without its effect when seen from the long distance of the nave, was smashed by a bomb which fell through the choir roof. It has now been replaced by a splendidly executed *baldachino* (58), heavily gilded and partly resting on wreathed and twisted columns, of the type which Wren intended for the choir of the cathedral; it was finished in 1958 as a Commonwealth Memorial for the two World Wars. Though the lower east window seems a little awkward when seen beyond this canopy, the *baldachino* is in itself a fine piece of craftsmanship and looks well when seen from within the choir—which was the longest view of it intended by Wren himself. But from down in the nave it seems remote and hardly noticeable, and strongly emphasises how essential to the designs of Wren, as to those of the mediaeval architects, was a long cathedral's firm division into nave and choir which prevailed at St Paul's till the screen was removed in the nineteenth century. Behind this *baldachino* the cathedral's easternmost chapel has now been fitted up, with neo-Baroque panelling and altar rails adorned with dates of note in the histories of St Paul's and America, as a Memorial Chapel to United States Service men and women who fell in the Second World War.

Down in the crypt, where an attractive central group of Roman Doric pillars corresponds to the piers of the dome, are some fragmentary monuments from Old St Paul's and others from early in the history of the present building; among these last is a charming cartouche to Wren's daughter-in-law who died in 1712. The architect himself is buried in the crypt, as also is Nelson, with monuments near his tomb to two of his Trafalgar captains. From this time onwards St Paul's became a pantheon of monuments to officers who had distinguished themselves in the Napoleonic War. The artistic results, despite the eminence of many of the Greek Revival sculptors, are far from happy. Far better, in the nave, is Alfred Stevens's fine classical canopied monument to the Duke of Wellington.

NORWICH
The Cathedral Church of the Holy Trinity

The period about 630 marked the final conversion to Christianity of East Anglia, for at that time the Burgundian monk St Felix, who was its first bishop, established his see at the Suffolk port of Dunwich, now vanished beneath the sea as a result of coastal erosion. In 660 the great diocese was divided by St Theodore, and both Dunwich in Suffolk and Elmham in Norfolk were the seats of bishops till about 950; the bishopric was then united, with the church at Elmham (whose foundations have been excavated) as its cathedral. In 1075 the bishopric was moved to Thetford, but in 1094 was finally established at Norwich in accordance with the current policy of fixing each see in the principal town of its diocese. Herbert de Losinga was the first bishop of Norwich, a Norman Benedictine careerist said to have owed his early advancement to flagrant simony. The founding of a cathedral and a Benedictine monastery at Norwich, on a scale commensurate with the dignity of so famous an Order, was considered to have been undertaken as a partial expiation of former irregularities.

The foundation stone of Norwich Cathedral was laid in 1096, and the building of the Norman fabric, in two stages, seems to have taken some forty or fifty years. But about 1170 a fire broke out in the monastic quarters; it spread to the church and may have partly destroyed the central chapel which led out of the eastern ambulatory. Bishop Suffield pulled down what remained of this chapel, and replaced it about 1250 with a Lady Chapel built on a more generous scale and in the current Early English Gothic manner. This work, however, having fallen into disuse and disrepair after the Reformation, was destroyed under Dean Gardiner about 1580. In 1271 rioting broke out in the city against the monks, whose unpopularity had reached a climax under the fierce and truculent despotism of Prior William de Brunham. Something like a pitched battle took place in the area of Tombland which lies just west of the cathedral precincts. Many lives were lost, and the cathedral and its claustral buildings were set alight and severely damaged. A sentence of excommunication was passed on the city, and Henry III himself travelled to Norwich to preside at the trial of the leaders of the 'sons of blasphemy', as the rioters were called. Great sums were extorted from the townspeople to pay for the damage; the beautiful Ethelbert Gate, leading into the Close and profusely adorned with East Anglian flushwork in flint and dressed stone, was also eventually put up by the citizens as an act of reparation. Another great misfortune occurred in 1361, when the wooden spire and part of the central tower crashed down in a gale, severely damaging the eastern limb. This led to the building of the fourteenth-century clerestory, with its blend of Decorated and early Perpendicular tracery, over the presbytery. The church was finally fireproofed in the fifteenth and sixteenth centuries, by the construction, under Bishops Lyhart, Goldwell, and Nykke, of a superb series of stone-ribbed vaults over the nave, presbytery, and transepts.

Despite these alterations Norwich Cathedral, more than any English cathedrals save Durham and Peterborough, retains the appearance and characteristics of a great Anglo-Norman monastic church, while it is better still than the two just mentioned in the retention of its internal subdivisions and furnishings. The west front was at one time built to a fine four-turreted design like that at Rochester. It now has a large Perpendicular window with a beautiful fifteenth-century western doorway below it, but it was much reduced in beauty and consequence by Victorian restorers. A large detached belfry, or *clocherium*, once stood a short distance to the south-west of the church.

The long north and south elevations of the nave still rise like cliffs, scarred as it were by stratum bands of arcading and windows. The transepts were refaced last century with plain Norman fronts, and the southern one well shows how a literal refacing can rob a façade of its charm and character. The considerably restored Norman tower at the crossing is rich work, with horizontal bands of Romanesque arcading and unusual vertical designs, composed of circles and diamond-shaped figures, between the windows of the main stage. More roundels, in vertically planned groups, occur in the top stage and at the corners are buttresses of vertical shafting which rise to fifteenth-century pinnacles at the four corners; the battlements between those pinnacles are charmingly adorned with panelling and shields. The tower is crowned by a tall stone spire(*60*), built late in the fifteenth century and forming a landmark over the low, gently rolling country which surrounds the city.

Easily the most beautiful part of the building is its eastern limb, with the lantern-like clerestory of the late fourteenth-century reconstruction rising high, with its lofty ring of later flying buttresses, above the close-knit Romanesque structure of the original presbytery whose apsidal termination and radiating chapels are of an intactness rare in England. The modern eastward addition, taking the place of the destroyed Lady Chapel but on a smaller scale, was built as a memorial to those of Norfolk who fell in the First World War. It is now the chapel of the Norfolk Regiment, with County Books of Remembrance for both World Wars, and a slab commemorating the men of the Regiment who died in 1951–1952 in Korea.

As one enters the cathedral the first impression is of the great length and height of the Norman nave(*61*). Its structure extends over fourteen arches on each side, arranged in seven double bays, and the great vertical shafts, in alternating designs, suggest that it was planned by its Norman builders to have a vault in seven double compartments, perhaps with a series of great cross arches as at Durham. The yellowish stone appears warm and mellow

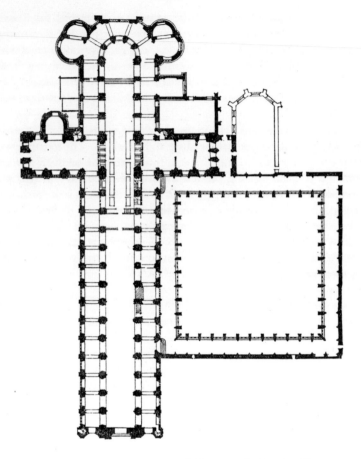

in the even lighting of the interior, and the general effect is of homogeneous texture and solid dignity. A remarkable feature of the design, perhaps dictated by requirements of lighting, is the great height of the single-arch triforium which equals that of the main arcade. Despite its general uniformity of planning this nave can show occasional variations in design; particularly the pair of cylindrical piers, with their spiral decoration, which occur at the ninth bay from the west and mark the original western termination of the cathedral as started by Bishop de Losinga. Other changes occur, on the south side, in the two bays reconstructed by Bishop Nykke so that his own tomb and chantry could go under the arches of the arcade. The arches themselves were changed to a richly decorated late Perpendicular design, while the two corresponding bays of the aisle were altered to allow more light and a richer scheme of panelled stonework. The aisles, now fitted with Decorated or Perpendicular windows, are covered by Norman groined vaults which contrast with the graceful lierne vault of the actual nave. This lierne vault ranks high among the achievements of late mediaeval mason-craft. It was built late in the fifteenth century by Bishop Walter Lyhart (1446–1472) whose rebus of a stag lying in water appears at the top of every other vaulting shaft. A striking feature of this vault is its profusion of sculptured bosses, now touched with colour, which run along the length of the roof in three ranges, and which illustrate Biblical history from the Creation to the Apocalypse.

The organ screen, effectively and properly dividing the nave from the choir, is a modern adaptation. It is surmounted by an organ case, in the Restoration style, which was set up, in 1950, to replace one destroyed by fire. At the crossing, the inside of the tower has three tiers of exceedingly fine Norman arcading, while the walls of the unaisled transepts (whose vaults are the early sixteenth-century benefaction of Bishop Nykke) continue the three-storeyed design of the presbytery and nave; many of their windows were reconstructed in the fourteenth or traceried in the fifteenth century. Between the transepts and the presbytery aisles the round-headed arches have been filled with beautiful screens of open Perpendicular tracery erected under Prior Catton about 1509.

The presbytery (62), without question, is the finest part of the cathedral. The side arcades were altered in the Perpendicular manner, in the same way as Bishop Nykke's two arches in the nave but earlier and in a slightly less ornate idiom. Under one of these remodelled arches is the fine tomb of Bishop Goldwell (1472–1499). In the apse, however, the Norman design still extends through both arcade and triforium. In its central arch, behind the high altar, the bishop's throne, alone of all episcopal thrones in England set in this basilican position, has recently been reinstated at its original height, up a flight of eleven steps and commanding a view down into the choir. Above the triforium rises the lightly poised clerestory of Bishop Percy's time, with its great glazed areas of window admitting a flood of light. It is remarkable how this fourteenth-century transformation blends with the Romanesque, and the whole with Bishop Goldwell's lierne vaulting.

The ambulatory round the apse forms a continuation of the groined presbytery aisles. From it open some chapels and chantries. Of these the most interesting are the two remaining chapels of the Norman east end which are so conspicuous a feature of the external design. Each is formed by two segments of a circle, and in the Jesus Chapel traces of original painting have formed the basis for an unattractive reconstruction of the mediaeval polychrome scheme. Mediaeval painting of far greater importance, and of outstanding beauty, is seen in the late fourteenth-century painted panels in the Chapels of St Luke and St Saviour. They were not originally in the cathedral, but were parts of altarpieces or screens in local parish churches. They have now been set up as altarpieces or separate panels, and are among the greatest treasures of any English cathedral.

The post-Reformation monuments, though numerous, are none of them in the front rank as works of art. Chantrey's seated figure of Bishop Bathurst (d. 1837) is, however, a dignified work, while several of the murals are of considerable Baroque or 'Adamesque' merit, including some of the late eighteenth century by the local designer John Ivory.

The cloisters are on the south side of the nave, and the fourteenth-century Prior's Door which leads to them is very stately and ornate, with canopied figures of saints and bishops unusually arranged in a radiating pattern round the actual arch. The spacious cloister walks have tracery of several periods from early Decorated to Perpendicular. The walks contain much of interest, including the monks' canopied book recesses and *lavatorium*. But their best feature is the great series of sculptured bosses in the rib vaulting; not long before the Second World War these were cleaned and touched with colour like those inside the cathedral. They are outstanding both for the quality of their sculpture and for the variety of their pictured scenes. The fine early Decorated chapter-house arches survive, but the chapter-house itself was pulled down by the Elizabethan Dean Gardiner. Some late Norman infirmary pillars remain, however, and the Choir School of the twelfth and thirteenth centuries, with a ribbed stone vault, remains and is worth a visit. The Close contains some beautiful Georgian and earlier houses and is entered from Tombland by two gateways which show the Norfolk flint flushwork. The Ethelbert Gate we have already noted. The tall-arched Erpingham Gate, by the Norwich mason James Woodrove who completed the west and north cloisters, was built about 1420 by the gallant old knight Sir Thomas Erpingham who appears, at Agincourt, as a character in Shakespeare's *King Henry V*.

60   *Norwich from the south-east. Norman south transept, 1096–1120; tower, c. 1121–45; Perpendicular clerestory of the presbytery, c. 1362–69, perhaps by Robert Wodehirst; flying buttresses, c. 1472–99; spire late fifteenth century*

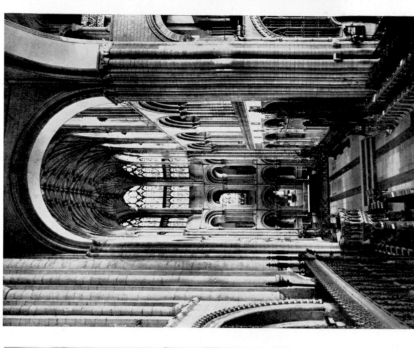

62 *Norwich: the choir and apse, 1096–1120, showing the clerestory,*
c. 1362–69, and lierne vault, c. 1472–99

61 *Norwich: the Norman nave, 1121–45, with its fifteenth-century lierne*
vault, c. 1463–72, possibly by John Everard

OXFORD

The Cathedral Church of Christ, formerly St Frideswide's

Though the virginal struggles of St Frideswide are largely legendary it is historically certain that this saintly Mercian lady lived in Oxford and founded a priory there about 735. This eventually settled down in 1122 as an Augustinian house with Guimond as prior. It seems that the original Saxon church, of which no certain traces survive, was burnt over the heads of a party of marauding Danes about 1000, and that after considerable enlargements and reconstruction the relics of St Frideswide were translated to the present building about 1180. The Lady Chapel was added in the thirteenth century and the Latin (properly St Catherine's) Chapel followed a century later. The choir vault is rather later than 1480. Early in the sixteenth century Wolsey tore down the three western bays of the nave to build the great quadrangle ('Tom Quad') of his new Cardinal College, and, but for his disgrace in 1529, the rest of St Frideswide's would probably have followed, to be replaced by a great new chapel which might have surpassed even that of King's College at Cambridge. Under Henry VIII the surviving part of the priory church became the cathedral of the new diocese of Oxford; the original plan was to use the far larger abbey church of Oseney whose great bell still tolls out as the famous 'Great Tom'.

The cathedral as it stands can be described as the smallest, shyest, and squarest of our 'greater' cathedrals. Yet it well proves that modest size need be no bar to great architectural beauty and interest. It is hemmed in by gardens and by the Tudor ranges of Christ Church, of which College it is the chapel as well as being a cathedral. Its situation is therefore unobtrusive; from the green sweep of Tom Quad all that can be seen is the low, sturdy thirteenth-century spire rising above the east walk, while the truncated nave is approached by insignificant modern arches. One of these gives access to what is left of the small but beautiful Perpendicular cloisters of the Austin canons. The westward truncation of the church, and the addition of two chapels on its north side, results in an almost square eastward plan. The internal effect is thus unusual and at first puzzling, despite some fine cross groupings. Of the main Transitional Norman interior design the most remarkable feature is the arrangement of the arcades in which an illusion of height is obtained by building up the piers with their early foliate capitals, and by throwing over the small, blind triforium stage lofty, round arches which

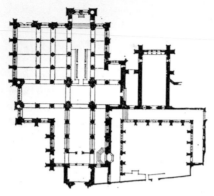

rise as high as the clerestory cill. The arches of the true arcade thus spring from half-way down the piers, being carried on small intermediate capitals which also support the vaulting of the aisles. The same device of gaining apparent height was used in the choir at Jedburgh Abbey and in two bays of the nave at Romsey. Here at Oxford there are various details, including pointed aisle vaults and clerestory windows, which show that the nave was built later than the choir.

The nave is ceiled with a good panelled roof, but the glory of the building is the design of the choir vault (*63*), a work of rare interest as showing the structural transition to fan vaulting. It is of a type which in Oxford had been employed with notable success a few years earlier in the roof of the Divinity School. In this the four-centered sustaining arches span the building in full view; at St Frideswide's they disappeared behind the pendents. The central space of the vault is patterned with cusped lierne ribs and bosses. It is clear from the clerestory in the north transept that the transepts too were to have been vaulted as in the choir. The east end, which once had a window of Decorated type with early eighteenth-century glass from Thornhill's designs, was lengthened and built up again by Scott with a large wheel window, and the sober Carolean fittings shown in Britton's view were replaced by Billings rather earlier in the nineteenth century. The thirteenth-century Lady Chapel is adjoined by the beautiful curvilinear Latin Chapel which has some excellent fourteenth-century glass, a complete range of stalls of the next century, and a Jacobean reading desk and pulpit. In this part of the cathedral are some notable mediaeval monuments and effigies, and what was once considered to be the watching loft of St Frideswide's shrine is really a fifteenth-century wooden chantry chapel placed on top of a contemporary tomb. The carved base of the shrine is no more than the piecing together of smashed fragments. It gives cause for satisfaction that any of the seventeenth-century windows by the Flemish brothers Abraham and Bernard Van Linge survived an outbreak of tasteless Victorian glazing. One must, however, say a word for the restful delicacy and pallor of Burne-Jones's work in several windows; one of these commemorates Dean Liddell's daughter Edith, whose sister Alice was immortalised by 'Lewis Carroll' who was a Christ Church don. Several of the cathedral's excellent Renaissance monuments are to members of the College, while others are to Bishops of Oxford. A third group commemorates eminent Royalists of the Civil War period when Oxford was the King's headquarters. A fine one by Jasper Latham is that of Lord Grandison who was killed in the siege of Bristol in 1643. It was put up after the Restoration by his daughter, then notorious as the Duchess of Cleveland and mistress of Charles II. Out in the cloisters the rectangular chapter-house, though entered by a late Norman doorway, is itself an excellent piece of Early English vaulted design.

PETERBOROUGH
The Cathedral Church of St Peter

The earlier history of the Benedictine monastery of St Peter forms a remarkable parallel to that of Ely. Situated on the edge of the Fens, it was founded by Saxulf about 655 and owed its subsequent growth to the conversion to Christianity of Peada, King of Mercia. Medeshampstede (the homestead in the meadows) was the first name given to the settlement that formed around the abbey buildings, but, with the growth of the establishment through the Middle Ages, the more portentous 'Burgh of St Peter' was adopted. Until the coming of the Great Northern Railway in the fifties of the last century transformed the character of the place, it remained a remote and almost unique survival of the mediaeval monastic borough, quietly ruled by a dean and chapter, just as for centuries previous it had been ruled by its abbot. As at Ely, the original establishment was sacked and gutted by the Danes about 870. It was rehabilitated some hundred years later under Edwin, when a new church was built, very splendid for its period. With the Conquest, a Norman abbot was appointed to St Peter's, which, like Ely, had its secular importance as an outpost for the supervision of the unconquered Fens; during the last phase of his resistance, the Abbey was attacked by the Saxon patriot Hereward, with a mixed band of Danes and English, who destroyed all but the church where he himself had taken the vows of knighthood. Not many years later this too was damaged beyond repair in a fire; but its reconstruction on a far larger scale and in its present form was undertaken almost immediately under Abbot John of Sais, the foundation stone being laid in 1118.

The building of the Norman Minster occupied roughly eighty years, during which time the work was continued by leisurely stages in general accordance with the original design, notwithstanding the momentous changes in construction and ornament that accompanied the transition to Gothic. It is doubtful that the church was ever completed with a Norman west front, but it seems certain that towards the close of the twelfth century the nave was extended westwards, and given western towers and a pair of short transepts to flank them. Then in the period about 1194 to 1210, under Abbots Andrew and Acharius, the west end of the church was completed and the striking screen front was added; there is, however, not the smallest reference in the chronicles to its building. The work must, however, have been completed by 1238, for in that year the abbey church was finally consecrated by the famous Grosseteste, Bishop of Lincoln in whose diocese Peterborough then lay. About 1272 to 1286 a sumptuous Lady Chapel was built, as later at Ely, in a position east of the north transept. This has not survived, and the last considerable addition to the church was made at the end of the fifteenth century and early in the sixteenth, when John Wastell's 'New Building', or retrochoir, was erected under Abbots Ashton and Kirton. Soon afterwards the reign of the abbots ended, and in 1541 the abbey church became a cathedral, perhaps owing its preservation to the presence, on one side of the presbytery, of the tomb of Catherine of Aragon who had died in 1536 at Kimbolton not far away. Another important royal funeral in the cathedral was in 1587 when Mary, Queen of Scots, was first buried there after her execution at Fotheringhay; she was later reinterred in Westminster Abbey, by order of her son James, when he had united the crowns of Scotland and England. Peterborough Cathedral seems to have fallen into considerable disrepair under the Stuarts, and with the Commonwealth was subjected by Parliament's troops to one of their most callously destructive outbreaks of iconoclasm, in which monuments, chantries, furniture, and indeed every malleable fitting, were smashed or mutilated beyond repair, and even the fabric of the church shaken. Towards the end of the century it was necessary for the townsmen to demolish the Lady Chapel and sell the materials for funds to effect urgent structural repairs; and despite the loss to architecture, it is to their credit that sufficient local affection remained for the great building to save it from otherwise inevitable decay.

64 *Peterborough: the fan-vaulted retrochoir, c. 1496–1508, by John Wastell*

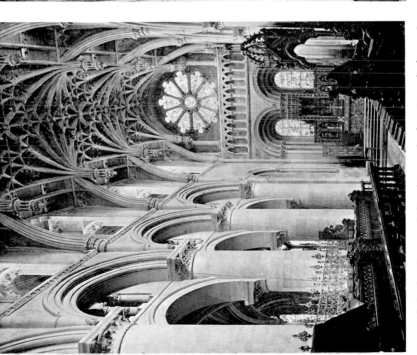

63 *Oxford: the choir, 1158–80, showing the late Perpendicular vault, 1478–1503, possibly by William Orchard*

65   Peterborough: the west front, c. 1193–1220, with the Perpendicular porch, c. 1375

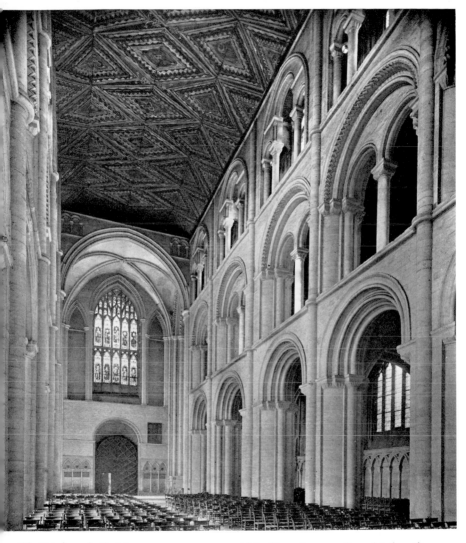

66   *Peterborough: the Norman nave, c. 1155-75, with its thirteenth-century diapered timber ceiling*

67   *Ripon from the south-east, showing the towers and the east end of the choir, 1288-97*

68   *Ripon: the choir, mainly c. 1154-81, and the east end, c. 1288-97*

Today little remains of the secluded cathedral city, where sedan chairs were still to be seen about the precincts in the forties of the last century; modern Peterborough has emerged as a railway and manufacturing centre, of which the Close forms merely a quiet backwater. In spite of the flatness of the surrounding country, the cathedral does not stand out boldly above the landscape as at Ely, but lies squat and low, though there are pleasant views of it from the flats to eastward, towards the ruined sister-foundations of Crowland and Thorney. At close range, the elevations of nave and transepts are unremarkable as façades, and tell a not unusual story of Norman arcading and fenestration adapted and enlarged to the lighting requirements of later periods. The low fourteenth-century central tower was rebuilt by Pearson, and the short eastern limb retains the original apse, with the addition of large blunt-headed curvilinear windows. Here an unusual effect is produced by a semicircular Norman upper storey rising above the square-ended lower stage of the late Perpendicular 'New Building', that forms the actual eastern termination of the church. But easily the most striking feature of the exterior is the west front (65), an astonishing *tour de force* of thirteenth-century design, incorporating three immense portals that emulate or even outvie the sculptured caverns of the Ile de France. A possible criticism would be the comparative slenderness of the flanking towers, with their fourteenth-century spires. Of the two towers of the western transepts that were to rise behind the screen, only one was completed, and this has lost its wooden spire. The gables over the portals include wheel windows and preserve much of their original sculpture, but some of the figures were recently found to be so decayed that they have been replaced by modern statues. The whole design is of an audacity and greatness of conception certainly more effective than the rather heterogeneous compromise of the Lincoln façade; and it is interesting to compare its treatment with the west-country plasticity of the work at Wells. The small late fourteenth-century porch placed within the central arch is something of an intrusion, though useful for the stability of the arch. Yet it hardly seems to detract from the equilibrium of the design as a whole.

The long, magnificent Romanesque nave (66) of eleven bays is dignified and well proportioned, with a slightly more elaborate treatment of the triforium and clerestory than at Ely or Norwich. With some fairly important modifications of design in the piers of its arcades, it continues, in its main elements, the design of the earlier choir and transepts and reveals the ingrained conservatism of twelfth-century Benedictine building. The main body of

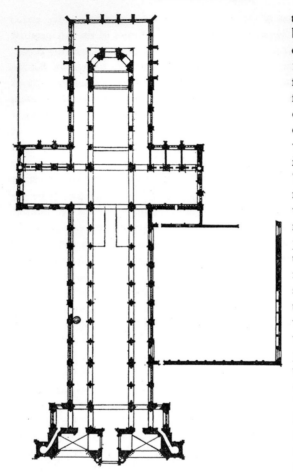

the work at Peterborough was not completed until 1193, and it is significant to compare its final phase with the design of St Hugh's choir at Lincoln, which is practically its contemporary. The aisles, with their ranges of interlaced wall-arcading, are roofed with quadripartite vaults, but the nave itself was never vaulted in stone, and retains the original canted wooden ceiling — a work of great interest, preserving its contemporary painted diaper decoration. The western door into the cathedral is one of the earliest specimens of English church woodwork, ornamented with a giant lattice pattern incorporating an archaic carved capital in the centre.

In their severe simplicity, the transepts are among the most effective features of the cathedral, each with eastern chapels which incorporate fifteenth-century screenwork of local type. They were ceiled in wood, and the chapels terminate in Perpendicular windows filling the Norman apertures. The shortness of the presbytery, though consistent with normal Romanesque basilican design, is something of a disappointment. Like the nave and transepts it has a timber ceiling, but in this case of the late fourteenth century

with bosses, and with half vaults of lierne type at the sides. The apse, however, is flat-roofed and is lit by a double range of curvilinear windows, of
which the topmost retain their old glass. The mediaeval *pulpitum* has disappeared and the stalls, replacing those put in by Blore in the 1820s, are
modern. The tessellated marble pavement was laid down last century, and
Pearson's Gothic *baldachino* over the high altar is inappropriate in an English
cathedral. The only early fittings are the fifteenth-century brass eagle lectern,
the panelled chest in the south transept, and the small double-piscina in
the south aisle, which has its counterpart in the south-western chapel.

Some of the best work in the cathedral is in the late retrochoir (*64*). No
original glass remains in its tall Perpendicular windows, but these admit a
flood of light to the interior, giving effect to the decorative elegance of the
stone panelling, with its range of devices that include the Tudor rose and
portcullis, cross-keys and croziers, and the rebuses and ciphers of the abbot
builders. The whole is roofed by one of the finest fan-vaults in England. In
this, the central bosses between the fans are each of them over a ton in weight,
and are carved with a variety of similar devices, including St Peter's
keys.

Some graveslabs of Saxon and late Norman abbots remain in the church.
But the tomb of Catherine of Aragon, along with other pre-Reformation
monuments, was destroyed by the Puritans, and Peterborough Cathedral is
not rich in memorials of the later Stuart and Georgian periods. The chapter-
house was destroyed after the Reformation, and of the cloisters, only the
boundary wall and the stumps of the vaulting shafts remain, with traces of a
lavatorium on the south side. The Norman prior's door into the cathedral
is richly carved. Two ranges of arches of the thirteenth-century infirmary
are standing, a few built curiously into the fronts of later prebendal houses.
The Close contains some interesting old buildings and two fine gateways.

RIPON

The Cathedral Church of St Peter and St Wilfrid

The monastery of Ripon was founded in the seventh century by Celtic
monks from Melrose and Iona, but following the ratification of papal
authority in England by the Synod of Whitby it was bestowed upon the

famous Romanist St Wilfrid, himself probably a native of the district. From his travels in the South, Wilfrid had absorbed something of the culture of Italy, and his enthusiasm for building found expression in the basilicas of Hexham and Ripon, and in the adornment of St Peter's at York. It seems likely that the Saxon crypt of Ripon cathedral is the work of this period. In 678, Ripon was raised to a bishopric for a few years, but on the death of Bishop Eadhed the church reverted to its previous status, and was eventually re-established as a church of secular canons which it remained throughout the Middle Ages. It formed, like Southwell, a supplementary headquarters of the vast diocese of York. Its collegiate status, abolished under Henry VIII, was restored by James I, and in 1836 it became the cathedral of a new diocese whose main centre of population is in Leeds.

It seems fairly certain that Ripon Minster was rebuilt or remodelled by Thomas of Bayeux, the first Norman Archbishop of York, at the close of the eleventh century, though the Norman crypt and apse of the vestry are all that remain of this period. Late in the twelfth century, however, it was entirely reconstructed by Archbishop Roger de Pont l'Evêque, who had already inaugurated a considerable building programme at York. The new design, whose extraordinary interest was first pointed out by Sir Gilbert Scott, forms an unusual expression of the transition, at its most delicate form, from Norman Romanesque to English early Gothic.* The nave was built broad and without aisles, with the lower stage of the walls left plain. A tall blind arcade arose from the first string course, divided by vaulting shafts which are the direct precursors of the slender Purbeck shafts which became a characteristic of the thirteenth century. The clerestory, moreover, predicts its Gothic forms. Archbishop Roger's design can now only be seen in the transepts, in bays at each end of the nave, and in part of the choir; but its architectural importance is unmistakable, and it provides a remarkable insight into the aspirations of the Transitional builders towards a national expression in Gothic.

One of the smallest of England's cathedrals, Ripon stands on rising ground in pleasantly pastoral surroundings (67). It lost something in exterior effect by the disappearance of the three lead-clad spires which rose from the central and western towers, the former of which was reconstructed by Ewan Christian on the old lines. Scott's 'purification' of the west front, including the removal of the mullions and Perpendicular tracery from the thirteenth-century lancets, gave it a rather featureless air. The nave, with its

* The design resembles that of Nun Monkton (Yorks) Benedictine church.

Rochester: the Norman nave, mainly c. 1115–30

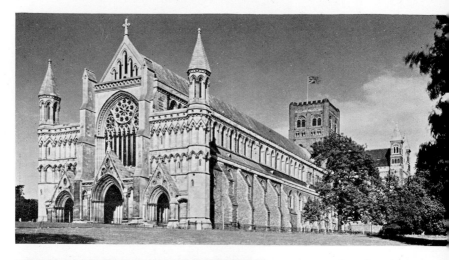

71 St Albans from the south-west showing the nave, the nineteenth century west front and the Norman tower, 1077–1115, by Robert Mason

72 St Albans: the crossing, 1077–1115, showing the reused Saxon balusters in the triforium of the south transept

ranges of large uniform windows, is mostly
a Perpendicular reconstruction as also, in
part, are the western bays of the choir. The
most distinctive part of the structure is in
the eastern bays of the choir which, with
its splendid Geometrical east window and
graceful flying buttresses, is finely typical
of the last phase of early Gothic in Yorkshire, as also seen at Guisborough and,
a little later, at Selby.

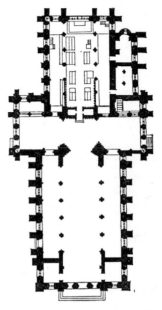

The interior, in which no less than six
building periods are represented, is a remarkable patchwork even for an English
cathedral. The nave, for the most part, is
a late Perpendicular reconstruction, but the
main features of Archbishop Roger's design are preserved in the two western bays
which now form the inner faces of the
western towers. Roger's work also remains
untouched in the north transept, but the south transept was altered in the
thirteenth century and remodelled in the fifteenth. After the collapse of
two sides of the central tower about 1450 it was found necessary to start rebuilding the arches of the crossing. This work was still incomplete at the
time of the Reformation and was then abandoned. This explains the eccentric
appearance of the western arch which has clustered Perpendicular casing
only on its southern side. The stone screen across the entrance to the choir,
with its beautiful canopied niches now filled by modern statues, is a dignified
work of the late fifteenth century, on a smaller scale resembling the choir
screen in the Minster at York.

The western three bays of the choir on the north side are Archbishop
Roger's work, and face across to three bays of Perpendicular reconstruction
on the south. The three eastern bays (68) continue with the Transitional
arcades, but above that level they are of a distinctive and homogeneous
Geometrical design of about 1290, with a glazed triforium and inner
duplication of the tracery screening the clerestory windows. The choir ends
eastward in a great Geometrical window of seven lights. The vault is a
passable reconstruction by Scott, incorporating some of the original carved
bosses. But the chief interest of this choir lies in its stallwork, executed by

the local craftsmen of the Ripon school and forming one of the finest achievements of late fifteenth-century woodwork. The two tiers of canopies, which include a good deal of Scott's work to replace some Jacobean canopies, are delicately designed and intricately carved, and there is a vigorous series of misericords, very charming in their treatment of scriptural subjects. The ornate stone sedilia, with additions by Scott, provide a touch of fourteenth-century exuberance.

The rectangular building between the choir and the south transept, apsidal in its lower storey, is used as a chapter-house and vestry. Except for the crypt it is the only portion of the cathedral that includes Romanesque work, though this was largely remodelled in Archbishop Roger's time. The low, massively ribbed vault probably dates from a few years later. The building is of three storeys, with an upper chapel, or Lady Loft, which was added about 1330 and is now used as a library.

The cathedral's monuments include some which commemorate deans and local magnates. Among the latter is an important one of 1789, by Nollekens, to William Weddell; its main design is modelled on that of the Choragic Monument of Lysicrates at Athens.

ROCHESTER
The Cathedral Church of St Andrew

The bishoprics of Rochester and London are, except for Canterbury, the oldest in England, having been founded by St Augustine in 604. Justus, one of the band sent by St Gregory to help Augustine's mission, was the first bishop of Rochester and the earliest church was dedicated to St Andrew, the patron saint of Augustine and Justus' monastery on the Caelian Hill in Rome. The foundations of the first pre-Conquest cathedral, a small aisleless building with a short apsidal sanctuary, have been discovered towards the west end of the present cathedral. The early history of this first Rochester Cathedral was one of incessant war and danger, but after the coming of the Normans the scarred Saxon building was finally demolished about 1080 by Bishop Gundulf, and a new church was begun for a choir of some twenty Benedictine monks. About forty years later this still uncompleted work was remodelled and partly recased under Bishops Ernulf (1115–1124) and

John of Canterbury (1125–1137). The new church was dedicated in 1130, but successive fires ravaged the interior during the twelfth century, and some years after one in 1179 the monks began the rebuilding and enlargement of the eastern limb and transepts. These were completed about 1240, but work on the fabric continued intermittently through the next two and a half centuries. The Civil War saw considerable spoliation of the fittings by Puritan soldiery, who 'so far profaned this place as to make use of it in the quality of a tippling place, as well as dug several saw pits, and the city joiners made frames for houses in it'. The mischief done at this time was, however, negligible compared with that worked by Cottingham and Scott, whose successive restorations, covering much of the nineteenth century, repeat something of the history of Hereford. Further work, particularly over the restoration of the west front, was done by Pearson.

Modest in appearance and moderate in its dimensions, the cathedral lies unassumingly on the edge of the old part of the city which is thronged with traffic and rich in its Dickensian associations. It looks north and east, along the Medway, towards Chatham and the old portions of its dockyard at the foot of a steep chalk hill. The nave, except for its fine arcaded west front which has been restored, after many vicissitudes, to its original, four-turreted design, has a plain Norman exterior with later fenestration and a plain fifteenth-century clerestory. The transepts are of the middle and later years of the thirteenth century, and the low central tower, quite appropriately designed in the Decorated manner, and with a blunt spire to crown it, was built in 1905 to replace a weak Gothic design by L. N. Cottingham. Above the fine Norman sculptured doorway of the west front (69), the large window is a Perpendicular insertion.

North of the choir stands the ruined shell of Gundulf's Tower, surviving (without its top stage) from the days when it was a detached belfry of the original Norman church. It is well seen, through a gap in the houses, from High Street. In the same view the four-way gables of the thirteenth-century eastern transepts are an unusual feature. The eastern limb itself, with its ambitious plan no doubt derived from that at Canterbury Cathedral, is Early English; in its north-eastern transept it contained the shrine of the pilgrim saint, the Scots baker St William of Perth who was murdered in 1201 on his way to Canterbury.

The nave's interior (70) shows Norman work of two periods. In the south aisle one sees the plain, unaltered arches of Gundulf's time. The rest of the Norman work, with pillars of varying design and chevron moulding

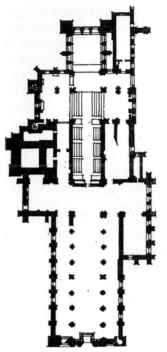

round the arches on their inner side, is more elaborate and is notable for the rich carving and diapering above the arches of the triforium. The clerestory windows and the impressive timber roof are of the Perpendicular period, and the two eastern bays were rebuilt about 1280, without any triforium, to an undistinguished design. Leading off the south aisle is the Lady Chapel, the only one so placed in any English cathedral and once also including the whole of the south transept. The part of the chapel which adjoins the nave was built early in the sixteenth century, with late tracery of an almost flamboyant character, and its interior would be much richer were it covered, as intended, by a fan-vault.

The choir, with its unusual feature of solid side walls which survive (as in a similar position at St Alban's) from the plan of the Norman church, is remarkably well enclosed and screened off from the rest of the cathedral. It is somewhat marred by an undue use of dark marble in the vaulting shafts and engaged arcading on these unpierced walls; and much of the beauty of furnishing and painting which it once possessed has been diminished by the Victorian refurnishing and bedizenment which replaced the simple Georgian panelling, throne, and stallwork which were put in during the 1740s. Some of the mediaeval wall-decoration survives, however, particularly one half of a splendid thirteenth-century Wheel of Fortune, while apart from the interesting early Renaissance desk fronts some wooden arcading of the thirteenth century is the oldest stallwork left in any English cathedral. The niches and statues on the screen were set up by Pearson to commemorate Dean Scott who collaborated with 'Alice's' father, Dean Liddell of Oxford, to produce the famous Greek lexicon.

Below the eastern limb the splendid crypt is partly Norman, but most of it is beautiful rib-vaulted Early English work. It thus has great distinction as the only large *Gothic* crypt beneath any English cathedral. The upper part of the eastern limb has an additional pair of transepts, and its design eliminates the triforium as does that of the choir at Southwell. Also like Southwell, the cathedral at Rochester is one of the few in England without a processional path behind the high altar, and a well-lit presbytery, with Decorated tracery inserted into the Early English lancet frames of the side windows, occupies the position usually held by an eastern chapel. Another striking piece of fourteenth-century architecture is the elaborate doorway, with statues and canopies round its jambs and arch, which leads into what is now the chapter-house.

The cathedral has an interesting series of bishops' tombs in good condition. Among them is that of Walter de Merton who founded Merton College, Oxford in the thirteenth century. The finest of these tombs is that of Bishop John de Sheppey, dating from about 1360 and long hidden behind later masonry. Of the later memorials, that of Bishop Warner (d. 1666) is a fine Corinthian work by the London sculptor Joshua Marshall, while other good monuments in the Baroque taste commemorate later members of the Warner family. The mural of Sir John Head (d. 1689) is an excellent work of art, with a portrait relief, by Grinling Gibbons, while of the Georgian murals the two large ones to Lord and Lady Henniker (d. 1803 and 1792) show important work by Banks and the younger Bacon, with statues of Time and Eternity in Coade's artificial stone on the lady's memorial.

Only scanty remains survive of the late Norman conventual buildings, whose position was unusual in that they lay south of the *choir* and not against the nave. The Norman entrances to the destroyed chapter-house are still, however, impressive. In the precincts Minor Canon Row, of 1721–1723, is a charming red brick early Georgian range, well showing how the terrace form could be used to serve the needs of a clerical community.

<hr/>

ST ALBANS
The Cathedral Church of St Alban

The church, a cathedral only since 1877, lies slightly apart from the town on a pleasant green slope. The red tinges in its fabric, most apparent in the sturdy central tower, result from the extensive use of Roman tiles and bricks from Verulamium. Thanks to the use of this brick, in preference to workable stone, by the builders of the great Romanesque church which was that of the premier Benedictine abbey in England, the work in general is of an unambitious, undecorative character (though the edges and under sides of the interior arches were eventually brightened by the use of painted banding and zigzag patterns giving a baldly chromatic impression like that of great Continental Romanesque churches such as St Michael's at Hildesheim). Yet the building is of great interest, and forms a remarkable patchwork in which almost every mediaeval style is represented. The present church was begun under Abbot Paul of Caen, between 1077 and 1088, to replace the Benedictine church which was said to have been founded by King Offa of Mercia in 793. There was the usual history of eastward extension during the thirteenth century, with the addition of a Lady Chapel in the current fashion. At 521 feet the cathedral is the longest in Europe with the exception of Winchester, whose eastern limb that of St Alban's resembles in its less ornate way. While its exterior design (71) is unpretentious, the west front and transept ends, created by Lord Grimthorpe late last century, provide a deplorable example of incongruous and opinionated revivalism. The west front and the great transept windows are the main items of his work, while the brick and stone transept turrets recall the worst efforts of German nineteenth-century pseudo-Romanesque.

Inside, the nave incorporates three distinct designs. First and foremost comes that of the Norman builders, heavy and archaic in character—like an immensely solid wall with its three series of plain arched openings. The three western bays on the north and four on the south side were added during the thirteenth century and have dogtooth ornament in the triforium and shafts for vaulting which was never built. Finally, after a collapse, five bays on the southern side were rebuilt about 1324 to 1327, to a design in general like that of the Early English bays yet clearly distinguishable from them. They have cinquefoiled arches and richer foliate carving, superb portrait label stops and the large shields of arms in the spandrels which recall those seen at York. This nave is ceiled throughout in oak, and has interesting traces of its original scheme of painted decoration, including some important panels of the Crucifixion, presumably intended to back small altars, on the western faces of six piers on the northern side.

The *pulpitum* is a stately structure of about 1360, and St Alban's is fortunate in retaining its clear subdivision between nave and choir; beyond it the stalls and throne are late Victorian work. The three bays of the ritual choir continue eastwards the Norman design, and the ceiling above them has fine heraldic painting of the Lancastrian period of the fifteenth century. The transepts are remarkable for the reuse in their triforium of turned Saxon balusters from the earlier church, with diapered Roman tilework in the tympana on the south side. The great arches of the crossing (72) are very fine and impressive in their architectural simplicity, and here the decorative chequering of the arches is at its most conspicuous and successful. Unfortunately the chapels which once projected from the transepts, providing the abbey with a striking many-apsed east end, were destroyed before the end of the Middle Ages. The presbytery was simply reconstructed in the thirteenth century, with the solid side walls of the original Norman presbytery and above it a fine timber vault which anticipated that at Winchester. At its third bay it is closed to the east by a stately reredos which was finished in 1484; it is similar to, but earlier than, those at Winchester and Southwark and was once rich in carved figures, now replaced by modern work. Flanking it are the beautiful late Perpendicular chantries of Abbots Wallingford and

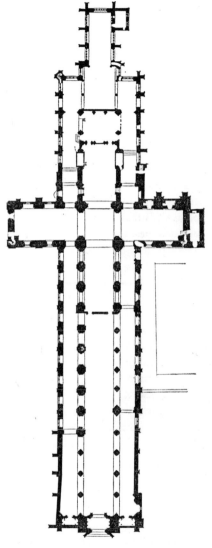

Ramryge. In this part of the cathedral we find an excellent collection of brasses, a type of monument in which St Alban's is richer than any other English cathedral.

In the feretory chapel behind the reredos stands the pedestal of St Alban's shrine; its fourteenth-century canopied work, and fragments of the marble twisted columns which once surrounded it, were patiently pieced together from fragments found in 1872. It is flanked to the north by a well-designed timber watching loft of the fifteenth century; this is faced by the large and stately chantry of Humphrey, Duke of Gloucester (d. 1447), the youngest son of Henry IV and a great benefactor to Oxford University. This chantry has particularly fine tabernacle work, pendents, and a miniature fan-vault. To the east of this chapel the late thirteenth-century retrochoir on the Winchester model has suffered appallingly by having once had a public passageway driven through it from side to side. The eastern Lady Chapel is a single-storey design of three bays, and for over two hundred years did duty as a Grammar School. It has since been very largely rebuilt. But the side windows are still for the most part of fine Decorated design, and the window splays with their charming little statuettes under crocketed canopies show how delicately the style of the fourteenth century flourished at St Alban's.

Except for the seventeenth-century breadshelves, the post-Reformation fittings and the monuments to parishioners are of no special note. Of the latter the best are those to the Maynard family and a Baroque composition, with two busts, to John Thrale, a London merchant who died in 1704, and his wife. At the Dissolution the fabric remained with the Crown till 1553 when it passed to the city and became, till attaining cathedral rank, the largest parish church in England. Some traces of the fourteenth-century cloister are visible against the south wall of the nave, but the other monastic buildings have wholly disappeared except for the great vaulted gateway to the west, dating from about 1365 and long used as a prison. In some ways it resembles the one at Ely, and like it is now used by a school.

SALISBURY
The Cathedral Church of St Mary

There is little that is obscure, or even very eventful, in the history of Salisbury Cathedral. In 1075 the see of Sherborne (with which the Wiltshire and Berkshire diocese of Ramsbury had been amalgamated) was moved to the ancient fortress of Old Sarum. For a century and a half a cathedral of much architectural interest, and in its choir of great splendour, stood there. But

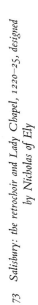

74 Salisbury: the chapter-house, c. 1263–84, by Richard Mason

73 Salisbury: the retrochoir and Lady Chapel, 1220–25, designed by Nicholas of Ely

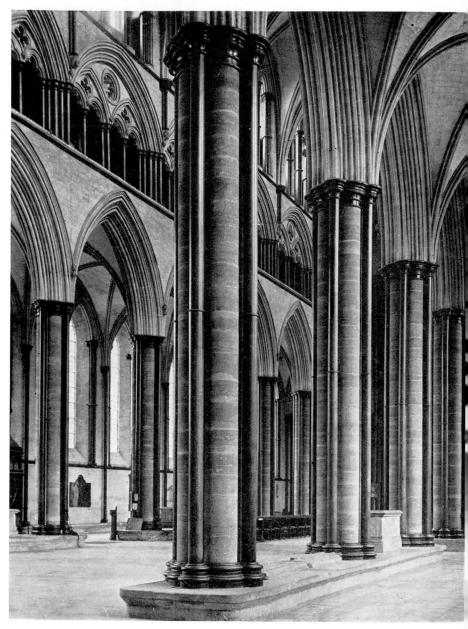

75 *Salisbury: the nave, 1237–58, from the south aisle*

76 *Salisbury from the south-east, showing the tower and spire, c. 1334, by Richard Farleigh*

77 Southwark: chapels of the retrochoir,
c. 1208–35. Probably designed by
Stephen Mason

78 Southwark: the choir, 1208–35, looking to the stone reredos, c. 1520, with
its modern statues

early in the thirteenth century the site was found to be so cramped, and in other respects inconvenient, that it was decided to build afresh on a new site two miles away. Work on the east end of the present cathedral was begun under the famous Bishop Poore in 1220. Nine years later Poore was moved to Durham, and with him went the canon Elias de Derham in whom some writers have recognised the architect at least of the earlier parts of Salisbury Cathedral; though from our improved knowledge of mediaeval methods it seems likely that his function was more like that of a modern clerk of works. Building operations continued steadily under Bishops Bingham, William of York, and Giles of Bridport, and in 1258 the building was consecrated with great ceremony in the presence of Henry III. The beautiful tower and spire were added in the first half of the fourteenth century, and with only the piers and light arches of the crossing to bear their weight they were a constant source of anxiety. They made necessary the building of many exterior and internal flying buttresses, and of the great strainer arches during the fifteenth century. The spire, and the whole of the remaining structure, were competently surveyed and strengthened by Sir Christopher Wren. In 1789 James Wyatt was employed on a general scheme of 'restoration' which included not only the demolition of the Perpendicular Beauchamp and Hungerford chantries flanking the Lady Chapel, and of the detached belfry which appears in old prints, but also a ruthless opening up of vistas and the destruction of the remaining stained glass. Not all these activities were wholly Wyatt's responsibility, but one may fairly say that on no cathedral did his hand fall more heavily. The work of falsification was by no means over, for in 1862 came Scott with an elaborate programme which left the interior with its present state of 'encaustic floors, varnished marble, and a choir bepainted and bedizened'. Some of the *grisaille* glass has been rescued and replaced.

The exterior, however, has largely escaped the restorers, and today the building appears much as it was left in the fourteenth century, in surroundings (whose smoothly green neatness is largely due to Wyatt) which are the most gently beautiful of any English cathedral; one can readily believe that here in Salisbury Close the novelist Trollope first had the idea which blossomed into the composite image of Barchester. The Close is itself an epitome of English house design at its best periods. Of the thirteenth, fifteenth, and later centuries is the rambling Bishop's Palace, while just outside the precincts Church House (once that of a merchant) is late mediaeval. Among a most pleasant group of the late Renaissance is

Mompesson House of about 1701 with its delicate iron gate and railings; it is charmingly typical of the middle-sized town house of its time. The actual cathedral, rising vast and shapely on its lawn, is one of the few in England that can be realised completely at the first glance and from many angles. But however varied the grouping, the general effect remains unchanged—of a lofty pile of warm-hued greyish stone, tinged with the green and gold of lichen, rising by stages to the slender grace of the central tower; and, exquisitely poised above all, the tallest and highest surviving mediaeval spire in England, the fame and glory of what Henry James called 'this blonde beauty among churches'.

This spire at Salisbury, 404 feet in height, is a landmark over miles of Wiltshire countryside. Constable loved to draw it as a central feature of his windswept compositions, and even the camera has not exhausted the range of viewpoints as we see it rising above the water-meadows west of the city. United in harmony with the Decorated architecture of the tower, its effect is beyond criticism, and the delight of one's first impression is amply borne out at closer range (76). If the main body of the fabric cannot aspire to this perfection, it does at least represent a complete and soberly expressive essay in the youthful style of the early thirteenth century; a realisation in warm Chilmark stone of its builders' stylistic aims and of their conception of an English cathedral's distinctive, unapsidal planning. The solidity and rounded curves of Romanesque had now given way to the sharp points and somewhat greater expanses of lancet fenestration, while the ritual arrangements which insisted on an eastern Lady Chapel and double transepts resulted in a multiplicity of façades which should have provided ample scope for decorative ingenuity. Yet despite its almost complete unity and cohesion, there is about the Salisbury design a lack of subtlety and a suggestion of repetition and monotony. Despite the lofty excellence of its proportions one finds a certain leanness in its ranges of lancets and gabled buttresses, with no more than a continuous arcaded parapet and the horizontal scoring of the buttresses to relieve an excessive 'verticality'. The west front, built later than 1258, was the last part of the exterior to be completed, and is one of the failures of its period. Designed purely as a screen it lacks much of the beauty and equilibrium of others elsewhere and remains a haphazard patchwork of buttress, arcade, and window, brought together with little sense of scale or texture, and with its niches now filled by poor modern statues.

The inside of the cathedral is less successful than the exterior. One must,

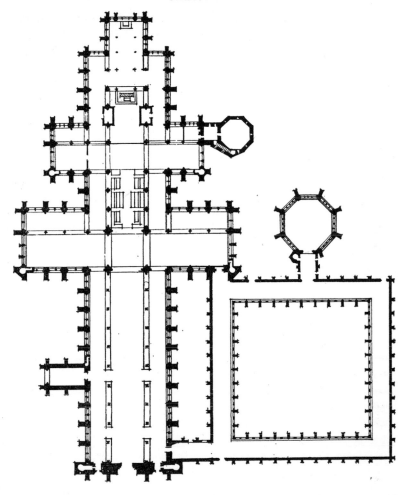

however, in fairness to its designers, remember that most of its screens and other fittings have been destroyed or moved elsewhere, and that much original colour has been lost by the smashing of almost all the old glass. Though far more uniform in its main design than any other English cathedral, this great church at Salisbury is not quite the same, from end to end, in all its details. The greater ritual sanctity of the choir and transepts is shown by the use of dogtooth decoration on their main arcades, while the later date of the nave is indicated by the greater use of foliate carving on such details as the corbels of the vaulting shafts and in the triforium openings. The thirteenth-century capitals, except for two in the choir which flanked the high altar, are simply moulded and Salisbury Cathedral, though by no means without its foliate carving, tended more than its contemporaries to reject the carver's services.

Swept and garnished by Wyatt and later by Scott, the lofty nave of ten bays gains its chief effect from its cool emptiness and perennial youthfulness. Technically it is a triumph of finished masoncraft, rejoicing in its use of Purbeck marble and deep-cut mouldings, the design being rendered throughout with flawless precision. It is impossible not to admire the smooth dressing of the grey piers of Chilmark stone (75), with their slender shafts and crisply moulded capitals of Purbeck, now darkened by varnishing. Above the arcades, the triforium with its wide arches has ample compositions of plate tracery and clustered Purbeck shafting, while between the triple lancets of the clerestory the vault springers rise to an even ridge line 83 feet above the floor; they thus make the vault one of the loftiest of its kind in England.

The tall arches of the crossing, on their slender clustered piers, would seem quite inadequate to carry the weight of the later tower and spire. One sees, however, that they are heavily strengthened by internal flying buttresses, while in the fifteenth century the masons, with their talent for decorative shoring, contrived, about 1460, the two beautiful girders, or strainer arches, of panelled and traceried masonry. Similar steps had been taken, in the previous century, to strengthen the entrance arches of the eastern transepts. Inverted arches, of a similar design to those at Wells, were built across the two openings, their side shafts being of stone (not Purbeck marble) and their foliate capitals of obviously fourteenth-century type. The lierne vault under the tower dates from the seventeenth century, but the original *pulpitum* was demolished by Wyatt, though important fragments of it can be seen in the north-eastern transept. His own screen, made up of fragments of the Beauchamp chapel, was in its own turn replaced by a spindly, unattractive metal affair by Scott and Skidmore. This Victorian screen was cut down to mere partition level in the spring of 1959; the loss need not be artistically regretted but one still misses the proper division between nave and choir which so long a cathedral should always have. In the full polychromatic horror of its painting and encaustic tiles, to say nothing of its Scott fittings, the choir presents an unhappy spectacle; but one finds some compensation in the excellent east window, by Pearson from designs by Mortimer and showing Moses and the brazen serpent in a vivid scene, which was inserted in 1781. A notable series of tombs and chantries has survived the restorers. These include the thirteenth-century canopied tomb of Bishop Bridport, with its arches and broken sculpture, and, on the north, the fine sixteenth-century chantry of Bishop Audley, with traces of original painting on its fan-vault; unlike his two-tiered chapel at Hereford it is of a single storey. The tombs of Bishops de Ghent (d. 1315) and Mortivall (1315–1329) have interesting iron grilles, and some good mediaeval ironwork from the Hungerford chantry was re-erected in the choir by Wyatt as a pew for the Earls of Radnor. Among a crowd of other and later tombs and tablets, mention should be made of the large and striking Renaissance monuments of Edward Earl of Hertford (d. 1621) and of Sir Thomas Gorges (erected in 1635 and an important specimen of Renaissance design), which now close the choir aisles to the east. Other monuments from this eastern part of the building were moved by Wyatt to the nave. They include some of early bishops from the cathedral at Old Sarum, and also the famous chain-mailed effigy of William de Longspée, the Earl of Salisbury who died in 1226 and was the first person buried in the new cathedral.

The retrochoir forms a single composition with the Lady Chapel (73), and was the earliest part of the building to be finished. One notices that there are no bosses and that foliate carving is almost wholly absent. The multiplicity of extraordinarily slender single and compound pillars which support the vault give an effect which is more curious than beautiful. The octagonal chapter-house (74), however, conveys a real impression of spaciousness, thanks to the slender delicacy of the central pier (with good animal carvings round its base) and the size of the Geometrical windows which almost fill each wall. Here also, in the spandrels of the thirteenth-century wall-arcade, is a prolific achievement of figure sculpture, providing some sixty little scenes of the Creation and other Old Testament episodes (9). The cloister dates from the same period (1263–1284), being simple but effective in its disposition of an arcade of uniform Geometrical windows beneath an expanse of plain wall. The fifteenth-century library is above one of its walks, and adjoining the south-east transept the little octagonal sacristy of the thirteenth century has a fine oak roof supported by a central column. The Close is entered by mediaeval gateways, and, in its eastern wall, one sees embedded much ornamented Norman stonework from the castle and cathedral at Old Sarum.

SOUTHWARK
The Cathedral Church of St Saviour

When Southwark was still a marsh, and before the building of London Bridge, the nunnery of St Mary Overy was founded under the wing of the Bishops of Winchester, in whose large diocese Southwark lay till Victorian times. It was later transformed by St Swithun into a college of secular priests. In 1106 Augustinian canons were installed, and they continued to serve the church till the Reformation. The fabric includes some Norman work, particularly in the north wall of the nave and on the outside of the modern Harvard Chapel, but the fabric emerged into its present state under Peter des Roches, Bishop of Winchester in the thirteenth century. Following a fire, he remodelled the nave, and later the choir and retrochoir, in the Early English style. After another fire in the fifteenth century, the south transept was rebuilt by Cardinal Beaufort at his own expense; a finely repainted achievement of his arms is a conspicuous feature in this part of the cathedral. In 1469 the vault of the nave collapsed, and was replaced by an oak roof from which 36 variously carved bosses are still preserved. After the Dissolution the building, though retained as a parish church (Shakespeare's brother Edmund being buried there in 1607), was allowed to slip into disrepair. This made necessary a series of drastic restorations in the thirties of the last century. Though the retrochoir was spared from a serious threat of demolition, the Lady Chapel was pulled down to make way for the approach to the new London Bridge, and a new nave was built to an emaciated design which greatly enraged Pugin. This, however, was duly demolished, and the present nave was started by Sir Arthur Blomfield in 1890. In 1897 the church was raised to collegiate status, and in 1905 became the cathedral of a new South London diocese.

As it stands today the cathedral at Southwark, a lovely masterpiece of early Gothic architecture amid the dinginess of its surroundings, is one of the miracles of London. It lies low by the river near London Bridge Station, hemmed in by noisy railway tracks and by a jumble of Dickensian warehouses to the west and north. The exterior has been almost entirely renovated, but a few original features remain; they include a thirteenth-century south doorway, some windows of Geometrical tracery, alternating with lancets, and a plain but dignified Perpendicular central tower, with its chequerwork parapet and slender corner turrets. Inside, Blomfield's well-proportioned nave closely follows the design of the choir, and resembles the original nave in its general effect. In its north aisle the fine canopied tomb of the poet Gower, a friend and contemporary of Chaucer who died in 1408, has now been set up and has recently been brilliantly recoloured in the mediaeval manner. The transepts, without the triforium stage, are picturesquely crowded with some good monuments to local worthies. Among them is an excellent Baroque mural to Richard Blisse (d. 1703), and a whimsical interest attaches to the florid tomb of Dr Lionel Lockyer who died in 1672 and was clearly, from his inscription, well known for his patent pills. The north transept contains a magnificent inlaid chest of 1588, and opening

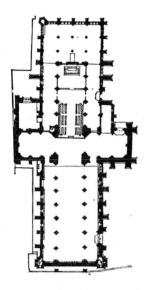

from it, through reopened Norman arches on the eastern side, the Harvard Chapel commemorates the Massachusetts University's founder, who was baptised in the church in the year when Shakespeare's brother was buried there.

The thirteenth-century choir (78), with slight differences of detail between its two sides, is a remarkably pure and beautiful piece of Early English design in five bays, with original roof bosses and simply vaulted aisles. It contains no old fittings, and the fine modern bishop's throne was designed by Bodley. The rich stone reredos, of the type he had already put into the choir at Winchester, was given about 1520 by Bishop Fox; its canopied niches are now filled with modern statues. East of it, the low rectangular thirteenth-century retrochoir (77), divided by clustered piers into four bays and twelve vaulting compartments, is perhaps the most attractive part of the cathedral. Its chapels are divided from each other by particularly delicate and beautiful screens by Comper, who did much to give Southwark Cathedral its present beautifully furnished appearance. Here too is a most splendid Holy Table of the late seventeenth century.

In general, the cathedral has a fine range of monuments and floor slabs. Among the former, one may specially mention the Jacobean group which includes the Humble and Trehearne tombs, each with its painted effigy accompanied by wives and progeny. Bishop Lancelot Andrewes of

Winchester (d. 1626), whose tomb is now south of the sanctuary, lies beneath a flaunting modern canopy of early Renaissance type. A word must be added on the magnificent brass chandelier of 1680 that lights the crossing.

---·∞∞∞∞∞∞·---

SOUTHWELL
The Cathedral Church of the Blessed Mary the Virgin

Southwell Cathedral, like that at Ripon, originated as a collegiate church served by secular canons, and for centuries formed a supplementary head-quarters for the archbishop of the York diocese. The archbishops, Wolsey among them, frequently lived in the great Palace whose ruins lie close to the church, and the splendid alabaster tomb of Archbishop Sandys (d. 1588) survives to recall this lengthy York connection (*14*). According to Camden, who gives Bede as his authority, the first church on the site was built by Paulinus, the famous missionary bishop of York in the seventh century, and it is certain that about 956 King Edwy bestowed Southwell, along with much neighbouring property, on Oscytel the Archbishop of York. Early in the twelfth century the Saxon church (from which one vigorous piece of carving survives) was demolished, and rebuilt under Archbishop Thomas of Bayeux; the western half of the present fabric dates almost wholly from this period. The reconstruction of the eastern limb was begun early in the thirteenth century and completed about 1250, and the exquisite chapter-house, one of the flowers of English middle-Gothic, was added about 1293. After various changes of fortune in the Tudor period, the collegiate status of the church lasted on till its extinction under an Act of 1840, and South-well Minster became a cathedral in 1884. It is an immensely impressive building in its setting of a quiet little country town which is hardly larger than a village.

Today, the most striking exterior feature of the Minster is its west front (*79*), to which the two conical spires, rebuilt during the last century and capping the sparingly arcaded, slightly differing Norman towers, give a somewhat Rhenish air. Between them is a large Perpendicular window of seven lights. The rugged design of the nave and transepts, crowned by a low, arcaded central tower, is relieved by such expressive touches of detail as the cable and billet mouldings of many of the windows, the string course of

79 *Southwell from the north-west. Transepts and nave, 1108–50; chapter-house, c. 1293–1300;
west window, c. 1450; conical spires of west towers rebuilt in nineteenth century*

80 *Southwell: the Romanesque design of the nave, 1108–50*

81 *Southwell: the choir,* c. *1230–50, with a glimpse of the screen,* c. *1330*

bold zigzag ornament below the aisle windows (some of which are fifteenth-century Perpendicular to admit more light), the unusual circular windows of the clerestory, and the incised patterning in the transept gables (which may be compared with that on the Norman gables flanking the western towers at Lincoln). The transepts originally terminated in apsidal chapels, while a little to the east of the northern one is the octagonal chapter-house with its conical roof; its delicate stonework was in 1959 under considerable renovation. The choir, with its miniature eastern transepts and foreshortened aisles, is a design of lancets and buttresses which terminate in steep-pitched *gablettes*. The Norman north porch, with its fine inner doorway, is of bold projection and is arcaded inside; the western pinnacle is really a chimney for the sacrist's upper chamber which has a fireplace and built-in cupboards. It was decreed that 'he should lie within the church, to be at hand to ring the bell at the right time'.

The interior of the Norman nave (*80*) has a certain solid effectiveness, with its arcade of squat cylindrical piers and simple rolled arches, its cavernous and somewhat ugly single-arch triforium, and its rather stunted clerestory, of circular windows behind rear arches of the ordinary Norman shape, which admit little light. The aisles are covered by simple quadripartite vaults in oblong compartments, and as at Norwich the triforium forms a virtual second storey of full aisle width. The central nave itself was never roofed in stone, the present waggon-roof having been added by Ewan Christian during the last century.

The crossing arches, with semicircular or clustered piers and with giant cable mouldings, are tall and effective, while the transepts have fine Norman arcading along their end walls and at triforium level. The stone choir screen built about 1330, is among the most beautiful of its type in England. The eastern and western sides are entirely different in design. The eastern, with its double tier of cusped and crocketed openings, is somewhat the richer of the two, and the whole screen is remarkable for its foliate and figure carving, the latter including many grotesque little animal or human heads, of which some of the latter might almost have served Gillray as models for his savage caricatures. The vaulting of the passageway has the rare 'flying' ribs also seen at Bristol and St David's.

The thirteenth-century choir (*81*), though somewhat low, has great dignity and simplicity which place it high among its period's achievements. The carefully calculated design, like that of the eastern limb at Pershore Abbey, dispensed with a fully developed triforium, and the tall inner arches

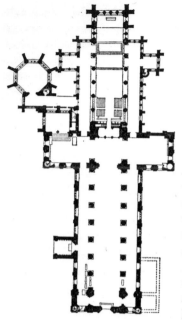

of the clerestory stage rise immediately above the arcade. Below the actual lancets, which are really too small to admit much light, blind arches on the wall take the place of a triforium. Lincoln influence is apparent in the rich corbels of the vaulting shafts and in the low springing of the vault, yet the composition is so effective in its proportions, so aristocratic in its quiet reserve of moulding and beautifully preserved detail, that it produces an effect of spacious serenity and calls to mind its great prototype. The unaisled eastern bays, with their magnificent late fourteenth-century sedilia, are lit by a greater array of lancets. Like Lichfield, Southwell has been much enriched by foreign glass made available at the time of the French Revolution and brought to this country early last century, and the four lower lancets in the east wall are filled with some magnificent French glass of the early sixteenth century. In the choir itself, the fittings are for the most part creditable late Victorian work, but the fine brass eagle lectern dates from about 1500 and was originally at Newstead Abbey.

The chapter-house is entered from its arcaded vestibule by a beautiful doorway of open tracery; the figure sculpture in the vestibule itself includes vivid heads of a bull, a monkey, and a dog. Octagonal in plan, the chapter-house's stellar-vaulted roof is a triumph of Gothic masoncraft, as at York dispensing with a central pier, though here at Southwell the work is of stone throughout. On the lower walls the continuous trefoiled and gabled arcading is of a magnificent elaboration in the carving of capitals, crockets, and spandrels—one of the most remarkable naturalistic displays of sculpture to be found in England. The carvers, though unknown by name, were probably familiar with somewhat similar work done at York and Lincoln, but the work breathes a stronger personality than anything else of this period, and there is a new imaginative freedom in the rendering of foliage in endless variety, and of bird and animal forms, with an almost uncanny skill in undercutting. This ornament is applied in freely rendered clusters and other groupings, which are the antithesis of the stiff-leaf formality of early thirteenth-century carving, and possible trivialities in conception are outweighed by an astonishing virtuosity in execution.*

Apart from the ruined Archbishop's Palace, another building of much merit in the precincts is Vicars' Court, rebuilt in 1779 as a charming three-sided composition in mellow Georgian red brick.

∞∞∞∞∞

WELLS
The Cathedral Church of St Andrew

Traditionally the first church of St Andrew at Wells was founded in 705, but nothing is historically authentic before 909 when the new see of Somerset was fixed here beneath the Mendips. The cathedral church was soon built in stone, with some quasi-conventual buildings to house its secular priests. It probably survived till the reign of Stephen, when Bishop Robert of Lewes (1136–1166) set about its replacement with such vigour that a great Norman building was ready for consecration in 1148. But this church was short-lived. Little is known of Bishop Reginald de Bohun (1174–1191), save that he was a friend of St Hugh whom he persuaded to come to Witham near Wells as prior of England's first Charterhouse. But it is practically certain that the construction of the building in its present form was largely carried out under this bishop, and done on artistic lines so revolutionary that the Gothic maturity of its design at so early a period becomes a thing of wonder. This Wells design does in fact represent a precocious, successful West-Country experiment in Gothic which ranks with, and perhaps surpasses in revolutionary significance, the choir at Canterbury or the work of St Hugh at Lincoln (where he moved *c.* 1192). Till quite recently it was dated some fifty years later, to the episcopacy of Jocelin (1206–1242), who was only in fact responsible for the completion of the nave on the same lines as the eastern portion of the cathedral, and for the addition of the very different west front. The ground plan and elevation drew nearer to their present form under Dean John Godlee (1306–1333), when the central

* For fuller treatment of this sculpture see Nikolaus Pevsner *The Leaves of Southwell* (King Penguin Books), 1945.

tower was in the main completed, the chapter-house built on its earlier undercroft, and the Lady Chapel added (originally as a separate building) in the form of an elongated polygon. The transformation of the east end was effected, under Bishop Ralph of Shrewsbury (1329–1363), with the addition of the three eastern bays of the presbytery, the alteration of the older choir so as to resemble the newer work, and the building of the beautiful retrochoir which formed a link between the Lady Chapel and the rest of the church. Except for the two western towers and the early sixteenth-century fan-vault beneath the central tower, architectural work virtually ceased till the nineteenth century, when the restorations of Salvin and Ferrey wrought considerable mischief, including the substitution of the present 'slate pencils' for the decayed Purbeck shafting of the west front.

Though the building does not stand out in conspicuous magnificence like Durham or Lincoln, it is nevertheless one of the most beautifully set of all English cathedrals. It stands on the edge of a small market town, almost in the shadow of the Mendips whose wooded escarpment rises not far from the fringes of the Close. Its west front is approached across a lawn. On the south side of it lies the thirteenth-century Bishop's Palace, with its encircling moat and drawbridge. On the north, adjoining the chapter-house and the early Tudor deanery, is the grey backwater of Vicars' Close, built to house the vicars choral and forming one of our most complete mediaeval domestic ranges. There is an extraordinary charm and repose in the grouping of these ancient buildings around the cathedral church.

The most striking external feature of Wells Cathedral is its west front (82), which was finished in the main by 1239. In Professor Prior's words, 'it is easy to see such a work as no framework of merely architectural designing, but as a whole piece of sculpture, and to recognise its object as not of aesthetic composition but of religious presentation'. The Wells façade is in fact a great screen of tabernacle work, at the same time enveloping the free sides of the two towers. It was built to house the most remarkable display of mediaeval figure sculpture in England—saints, priests, and bishops, with kings, nobles, ladies, and characters of legend and scripture. The central gable is crowned by a mutilated figure of Our Lord in Glory, while beneath it a splendid range of the Apostles, practically intact, runs across above tiers of angels and a panelled representation of the Doom. Relief is provided by a range of six boldly projecting buttresses, which cast angular shadows and bring depth and texture to the composition. The buttressed towers, of similar design but with some differences of detail, are Perpendicular

2 *Wells: the west front, c. 1220–39, probably designed by Adam Lock. South-west tower 1365–90, by William Wynford; north-west tower c. 1410–35*

84 Wells: the strainer arches of the crossing, c. 1338, by William Joy

85 *Wells: the Lady Chapel, c. 1293–1319, from the connecting retrochoir of slightly later date*

86 *Winchester from the south-east. Tower 1108–20; retrochoir and Lady Chapel 1202–1235; presbytery c. 1320–60, altered early in sixteenth century; eastern bay of Lady Chapel c. 1490–1500*

additions and form a dignified architectural culmination to the rich variety of the earlier work.

The nave is plain in elevation, with a fourteenth-century pierced parapet above a course of ballflower ornament; similar cresting is seen round the rest of the cathedral. Perpendicular tracery has been put into the lancet windows, and on the north side is a boldly projecting Early English porch. The transepts are of comparatively shallow projection, and adjoining the northern one are the octagonal chapter-house, with its wide Decorated windows and a rich parapet, and the fifteenth-century bridge which leads across the road to Vicars' Close. The central tower, though of no great height, is among the most lovely in England and in its main design dates from about 1321. Though simple in general treatment, it is finished with an artistry of (slightly later) detail that commands our admiration. The east end, with the polygonal Lady Chapel and chapter-house, and with good flying buttresses to mark the later portion of the choir, is the richest part of the fabric, being designed with a broad elegance in its Decorated windows and other fourteenth-century detail. It can best be judged from the Mendip foothills which rise behind it; from them the view of the cathedral is of a serene beauty scarcely surpassed in England.

Within, the nave (3) is of ten bays, of which the eastern four represent Bishop Reginald's work. The main design is, however, continued all the way down but differs from that of the transepts in that the triforium on each side is made up of a continuous row of arches with carved roundels in the spandrels above, while the transept triforium has no roundels and its arches are arranged in disconnected pairs. With its closely spaced, rather massive piers, acutely pointed arches, and deep-cut mouldings, this early Gothic design has a solidity, without heaviness, that is relieved by the delicate perfection of the 'stiff-leaf' capitals. Some of these have interpellated figures and forms emerging from among the rich foliations. One can only mention a few famous examples such as the cobbler, the fruit stealers, and the man with toothache on a capital in the western arcade of the south transept.

The transepts, along with the arcades and some of superstructure of the three western bays of the choir, are the earliest parts of the cathedral, built by Bishop Reginald from about 1186. It is in the crossing (84), across the entrance arches to the nave and transepts, that we find the most distinctive features of this interior in the great inverted strainer arches which support the weight of the tower. They were made necessary, about 1338, by the dangerous settlement of the main piers. Their insertion was a bold, structurally successful expedient, which has been attributed to the innovating school of West-Country masons responsible for the open vaulting in the cathedral at Bristol, and later for the recasing of the choir at Gloucester.* The aesthetic success of these stone girders is a matter of opinion, but their sensationalism is beyond question, and a diagonal vista embracing the three great arches, with the open 'eyes' in their spandrels, at least provides a unique visual experience. Further support is also given to the tower by the insertion, into some of the arcade arches closest to the crossing, of narrower fourteenth-century arches whose moulded capitals are clearly of that period. The fourteenth-century screen, much altered by Salvin, is largely obscured by the three strainer arches. East of it, the choir(*83*) consists of the clearly different work of Reginald and of Ralph of Shrewsbury, each part being of three bays, but the whole being largely unified by the similar treatment which was given to the triforium stage in the fourteenth century, and by the building over the choir's whole length of a vault which is patterned with cusped lierne ribs, and whose proportions and detail are among the most effective in any English cathedral. The vertical treatment of the triforium is as remarkable as it is successful. It virtually forms a continuous range of tabernacle work, and in Bishop Ralph's three new bays the shafting drops right down into the spandrels of the arcade. In addition to the 'golden' Jesse window at the east end, four clerestory windows retain almost all their old glass, but except for the fourteenth-century misericords all the choir fittings are Victorian. The recently worked tapestry hangings behind the stalls and throne are of considerable beauty, and repay close inspection for their heraldry and other subtly allusive details.

The polygonal Lady Chapel(*85*), completed fairly early in the Decorated period, is one of the most exquisite smaller works of English Gothic, and, though mostly filled with a kaleidoscope of glass fragments, its tall windows still glow with something of their old richness. The vaulting dispenses with a central pier and culminates in a beautiful boss of Christ in Glory. As at Lichfield, this Lady Chapel was first a separate block, and its inclusion in the church was effected by a complex disposition of freestanding vaulting piers, with slender Purbeck shafts and somewhat weakly foliated capitals, in the present retrochoir. The vistas among the piers are of singular beauty, each terminating in a deep glow of colour from the chapel's windows.

* It is interesting that the nearby abbey church at Glastonbury soon had its choir cased in the Gloucester manner, and that in the Perpendicular period its tower was supported by inverted arches in the manner of Wells.

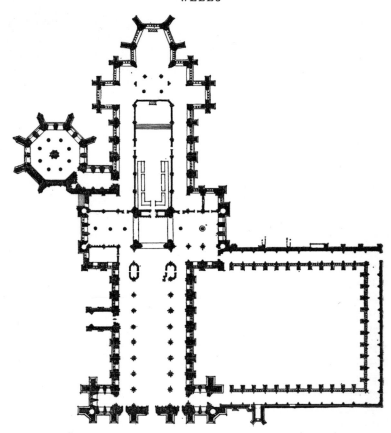

The feretory chapel remained untenanted, as two applications for the canonisation of Bishop de la Marchia (1293–1302) proved unsuccessful. The ends of the choir aisles and the small eastern transepts form a group of chapels which house tombs of bishops and others. Of these the cathedral contains a notable group, particularly those of Bishops Drokensford and Beckington, and the Perpendicular chantries of Bishop Bubwith (1407–1424) and Treasurer Sugar in the nave.

From the north choir aisle a passage leads to the thirteenth-century vaulted undercroft of the chapter-house; the upper storey is approached from the north transept where the astronomical clock, of about 1390 and with its outer face and clock jacks lately repainted in bright colours, is kept in order and provides a popular spectacle with its inner figures of 'Jack Blandiver' and mounted knights. Up the famous doubly branching staircase, the chapter-house is entered through a doorway of open tracery. Its interior is one of the most beautiful of its sort in any English cathedral, being lit by eight traceried windows which fill the upper parts of each wall and have fragments of old glass in their heads. The central pier is built of clustered shafts, and from the capital springs a branching growth of slender ribs, caught in ridge ribs and studded with carved bosses. The cloisters, without a northern walk, were built by Bishop Beckington in the fifteenth century, and the long library lies over their eastern range. Many Georgian monuments once in the nave are now in these cloisters. Among them is that which commemorates the Bath musician Thomas Linley (d. 1795) and his beautiful daughter Elizabeth who eloped to become Mrs Sheridan. The fine Baroque monument to Bishop Hooper (d. 1727) was by Samuel Tufnell of Westminster and cries out for restoration and replacement. In the cathedral itself the best post-Reformation monument is that to Bishop Kidder. He succeeded the saintly Thomas Ken and was killed, along with his wife, when a chimneystack in the palace blew down in the great storm of 1703. A splendid feature of the nave is the brass desk lectern, made by William Burroughes of London (who also made the lecterns at Lincoln and Canterbury) in 1661 and given by Dean Creighton who later became bishop. He also gave the seventeenth-century glass which fills two of the great lancets which make up the west window.

WINCHESTER
The Cathedral Church of the Holy and Indivisible Trinity

The history of Winchester reaches back beyond the Roman occupation, to a period when Caergwent, in its cradle of chalk downs, was the most considerable settlement of southern Britain. Here the Romans built *Venta Belgarum*, whose importance lingered through the centuries after their withdrawal till at length it emerged as the chief city of Wessex and later as the capital of the Saxon kings of England. The place's ecclesiastical history, as might be expected, is long and complex. The original Saxon church, the shrine of St Swithun, seems to have been enlarged under St Ethelwold about 963; he also added conventual buildings for the Benedictines. From now until the Conquest the monastery's affairs proceeded tranquilly enough, and it was not until 1079 that the first important chapter in the history of the present cathedral began with the demolition of the old church by Bishop Walkelin and his brother Prior Simeon (later Abbot of Ely), who started a vast building on typically Anglo-Norman lines. This was formally consecrated in 1093, in the presence of almost all the bishops and abbots of England. It was very massively constructed and its crypt, its core, and parts of its outer fabric continue to do service today. Apart from the reconstruction of the central tower which collapsed (according to the fable) when the body of the impious Rufus was laid beneath it, no further work took place till after the accession of Bishop de Lucy (1189–1204), who extended the church eastward by building a rectangular retrochoir. But the greatest period of building, which saw the virtual transformation of the western part of the cathedral, was schemed and tentatively started by Bishop Edington (1346–1366), to be continued on a more generous scale under the famous William of Wykeham (1364–1404), whose courtly prestige and beneficence were equalled by his enthusiasm as a builder. He was the founder of New College, Oxford, and of his own College at Winchester, and the cathedral nave is a splendid memorial to his architectural discrimination. Willis describes his achievement in his Winchester monograph. 'The old Norman cathedral', he writes, 'was cast nearly throughout its length and breadth into a new form; the double tier of arches in its peristyle [i.e. arcade and triforium] was turned into one, by the removal of the lower arch, and clothed with Caen casings in the Perpendicular style. The old wooden ceilings were replaced with stone vaultings, enriched with elegant carvings and cognisances. Scarcely less than a total rebuilding is involved in this hazardous and expensive operation, carried out during ten years with a systematic order worthy of remark and imitation.'

Wykeham's successors continued his tradition, and Beaufort, Waynflete, Courtenay, Langton, and Fox all added their quota to its splendours, not least among them their own tombs which form a splendid group to the east of the high altar. The fabric suffered little at the Reformation, but with the Civil War there occurred a terrible violation of the interior by Parliamentary troops who stripped its shrines, tore down its statues, and smashed nearly all its old glass. Nineteenth-century restoration was comparatively slight, but at the beginning of the present century signs of settling in the foundations necessitated a tremendous work of concrete underpinning, and the erection of the fine row of detached buttresses which replace the destroyed claustral buildings as a southern abutment to the nave.

Internally, Winchester Cathedral has survived as a vast repository of mediaeval craftsmanship, enshrining a crowded ceremonial chapter in the national history. Externally, it has to be admitted that its appearance is disappointing, and that even its situation is unremarkable in a city that contains as much of historic interest as any in England, including Wykeham's fourteenth-century College, Wren's Wolvesey Palace, the great hall of the Castle, and the unique mediaeval group of St Cross Hospital. By contrast, the outward plainness of the cathedral comes as something of an anticlimax, lying long and squat in a pretty Close of lime avenues and sleepy old houses (*86*). Edington's gabled west front of about 1360 replaces a Norman façade which stood several feet more to the west; it is a rather mechanical essay in the new Perpendicular style, but the recesses of its three doorways have delightful little lierne vaults and carved bosses. Except for the two western bays of its aisles, which are also Edington's work, and whose windows are of an earlier type than those east of them, the nave was heavily recast to a plain early Perpendicular design and is flanked by even ranges of stepped buttresses. The transepts retain their Romanesque severity despite some beautiful Decorated windows, and some Perpendicular tracery inserted into Norman window spaces. The plain, low central tower was probably surmounted by a leaded spire in the early Middle Ages,* but does not in its present form make an impressive culmination to the building's bulk. The eastern limb, as finally completed in the early sixteenth century, is the richest part of the fabric, with dignity and elegance in its transomed Perpendicular windows and in its crocketed Perpendicular pinnacles and flying buttresses of about 1520 by Thomas Bertie. East of the presbytery, the thirteenth-century retrochoir forms a low extension, terminating in the graceful Perpendicular Lady Chapel where the arms of Bishop Courtenay indicate a building date between 1486 and 1492.

Inside, the contrast with the building's external severity is immediate and impressive, and the view up the long, lofty nave (*87*) of twelve bays is as dazzling as anything in cathedral art. Here is one of the most eloquent works of English Gothic, a shapely and harmonious recasing which gives little stylistic indication of the massive core of Norman masonry inside it. Closely spaced and crisply moulded into a multiplicity of parts, the piers do not

* For this spire, see John Harvey in 'Winchester Cathedral Record', No. 27, 1958.

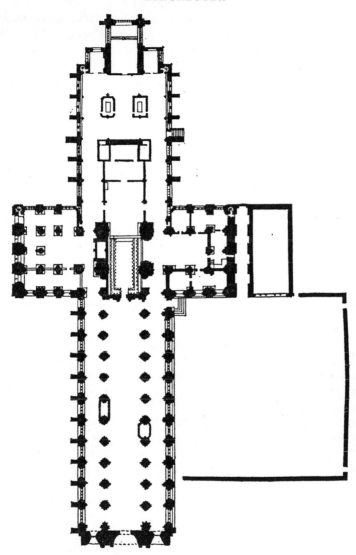

fully suggest their great solidity, and an insistent sense of height, due mainly to the fact that the Norman arcade and triforium were virtually combined into a single storey, is conveyed by the tall vaulting shafts which form the pillars' inner members, rising slenderly to the clerestory where small foliate capitals carry the springers of the complex lierne vault, whose heraldry indicates that it was not finished till after 1405. Characteristically Perpendicular are the panelled spandrels of the arcade; above them the 'triforium' is no more than an alleyway, and a series of pierced parapets carried on a cornice enriched with a fine corbel table of heads and floral bosses. The lower lights of the clerestory windows are filled with stone panelling. On the south side, the fifth bay from the west is filled by the delicately towering Perpendicular screenwork of Wykeham's chantry, in which the bishop's effigy is supported at the head by angels and at the feet by curious little figures of monks (16). Bishop Edington lies in simple dignity in the tenth bay; in the sixth bay from the west on the north side is the square Romanesque font of black Tournai marble, carved with early reliefs of the life of St Nicholas. In the three eastern bays of the structural nave, shafts and cushion capitals of the original compound Norman piers remain uncased and well indicate the skilful methods employed by Wykeham's masons.

In its archaic severity the Norman work of Simeon and Walkelin's transepts forms a striking contrast to the more ornate brilliance of the nave, and much resembles the work, started later under Simeon, in the transepts at Ely. It is on a tremendous scale even for its period and after the tower's collapse some portions were rebuilt with conspicuously superior technique, with narrower joints and ashlar facings. A curious feature is the aisle, continuous with those on the eastern and western sides, which runs along the end of each arm. It thus forms a succession of small groined chapels, with some interesting screenwork on the southern side. Both transepts have wooden roofs, and in the northern one, between the tremendous crossing piers, is the recessed chapel of the Holy Sepulchre with its extensive and important remains of mediaeval mural painting. The ritual choir, which partly extends into the nave, lies mainly under the crossing which is roofed with a timber fan-vault of 1634. The canopied stalls are very fine and intricate work of 1308–1310, with beautiful figure and animal carving and a charming series of misericords; it is typical of their period that the design is more akin to the stonecutter's craft than to that of the carpenter. The throne in the presbytery is clearly modelled on these stalls and is an interesting work from the episcopate of Bishop Tomline (1820–1827); it succeeds a canopied Corinthian throne erected by Bishop Trelawney (1707–1721).* The present

---

* The idea of a new throne, in its style assimilated to an existing set of mediaeval stalls, may have come to Bishop Tomline's mind from what he had experienced in his previous cathedral of Lincoln.

87 *Winchester: the nave, reconstructed by William Wynford, c. 1394–1410*

88 Worcester: the eastern
      limb, begun 1224.
      Designed by
      Alexander Mason

89 Worcester: the Norman
      crypt, 1084–92

90 *Worcester from the north-west across the River Severn. Tower c. 1360–74, by John Clyve; west front 1375–95, largely renovated in modern times*

91   York: the north transept, 1245–60, with its 'Five Sisters' window

screen, by Scott, is also an adaptation from the design of the stalls; its predecessor was an early nineteenth-century Gothic structure which replaced the magnificent Palladian screen of the early seventeenth century by Inigo Jones. The statues of James I and Charles I from the niches of this screen are now in the nave, and the central part of its structure is in the Museum of Archaeology at Cambridge. But some beautiful classical fragments forlornly remain in the crypt at Winchester itself.

Below the presbytery, the Norman crypt is of great interest and importance; as at Worcester it shows the ground plan of the work which once stood above it, and its undercroft of an eastern chapel projects further than such chapels normally did in Norman churches. The actual presbytery, a disappointing work, is of four structural bays, that east of the high altar being canted inwards to join the narrower retrochoir. The piers and arches are unimposing architecture of 1320 below an elegant pierced parapet. The timber vault, with its carved and painted bosses, is of the early years of the sixteenth century when the presbytery and its aisles were transformed and beautified by Bishop Fox (1500–1528) who inserted the stately stone reredos, with its intact canopies and modern statues, which is on the same lines as the one he gave at Southwark. The beautiful stone screens which fence off the aisles were also added by Bishop Fox, and are dated 1525; they combine delicate Perpendicular tracery with Renaissance cornices, which bear the six carved and painted chests containing the bones of the Saxon kings and bishops.

De Lucy's retrochoir, with its chamfered or moulded Early English detail, forms a setting for the series of tombs and chantries which are one of the cathedral's glories. Facing each other, and at one time having the shrine of St Swithun between them, the chantries of Beaufort (d. 1447) and Waynflete (d. 1486), the prince and the pietist, are very similar in design. Fox's chantry is of an elaboration that surpasses both of these in its wealth of carved detail, while the chantry of Bishop Gardiner, perhaps from about 1554 when he married Philip II of Spain and Mary Tudor in the cathedral, is of the highest artistic interest though not of outstanding beauty. Its late Perpendicular tracery recalls the design of Fox's screens, but its fluting, strapwork, and Doric frieze are fully Renaissance in treatment. So too, above a late Gothic interior ceiling, is the upper reredos of the interior which contains the chair in which Mary I sat during her wedding ceremony. Directly east of the high altar are the nine splendid fourteenth-century canopied niches of the feretory which contained the cathedral's relics, except for those of St Swithun. The Lady Chapel is a Perpendicular reconstruction and extension of de Lucy's early thirteenth-century work, whose elaborate arcading and panelling still appears in its first bay. Its most distinguished features are its sober wooden screens and stalls of the late fifteenth century. Flanking it are two small chapels. On the north is that of the Guardian Angels, with interesting roof paintings and Le Sueur's fine recumbent bronze effigy of Richard Weston, Treasurer to Charles I; the southern one is Bishop Langton's ornate and richly screened chantry, filled with elaborately carved woodwork of about 1500.

The cathedral possesses two very fine brass 'branches', or chandeliers, of 1756, and a great variety of excellent post-Reformation monuments in various idioms from Baroque to Greek Revival. Sir John Clobery (d. 1687) is commemorated by an Ionic canopy and a standing figure by Sir William Wilson, while in the nave the Palladian monument of Bishop Willis (d. 1734), with its reclining effigy, is an excellent work by Cheere(17). Among the 'Regency' monuments the Greek Revival sculptors Flaxman and Chantrey are both represented. But none of these later memorials exceeds in human interest the floor slab to Jane Austen, who died in 1817 in a house not far from the cathedral. Unlike Britton, the inscription makes no mention of her novels, but in its wording confines itself to 'the extraordinary endowment of her mind'.

WORCESTER

The Cathedral Church of Christ and Blessed Mary the Virgin

While Worcester was certainly the seat of a Saxon bishop from the seventh century, little is known of its history till 964 when St Oswald founded a new church there for Benedictine monks. In 1041 this was gutted by the minions of King Hardicanute, and in 1084 its rebuilding on a larger scale was begun by St Wulstan, who alone among the pre-Conquest prelates retained his position for many years after 1066. This second church had a chequered history. In 1113 it was seriously damaged by fire, and in 1139 there occurred the curious raid from Gloucester during which the entire population, with its belongings, took refuge in the cathedral church. In 1175 the central tower collapsed, and in 1180 much damage was done by a second fire. The building of the present church, above the level of the crypt, may be said to date from about 1170 with the construction of the two western bays of the nave to a remarkably advanced Transitional design. By now the fame of the canonised Wulstan had spread throughout Europe, and his shrine at Worcester became a favoured place of pilgrimage. In 1207 it was visited in state by King John, but, when in 1216 the city embraced the cause of the Dauphin Louis against that despot, his forces descended on it with considerable savagery, extorting so large a fine from the cathedral priory that the saint's shrine had to be melted down to raise funds. John, dying at Newark a few months later, left the caustic direction that his body should be buried in Worcester Cathedral between the shrines of St Oswald and St Wulstan, and it remains there to this day. The rebuilding of the eastern limb was begun in 1224 and work continued intermittently till in 1374 the building may be said to have emerged in its present form with the completion of the central tower. Surprisingly small damage was done to it in the fierce siege of the 'Faithful City' during the Civil War, but in 1651, after the Battle of Worcester, the city was again occupied by the troops of Parliament, who confined 6,000 prisoners in the cathedral, plundering and damaging the interior. The building was virtually abandoned until the Restoration, when services were resumed.

Despite the loss of its detached belfry, and despite restoration amounting almost to transformation of its exterior, Worcester Cathedral still stands impressively on the southern edge of a busy manufacturing and shopping town with its restful, dignified Georgian churches. The gable of its west front and the massive but delicate central tower form a fine composition from the green flats across the Severn(90). There is a story that when St Wulstan demolished St Oswald's work to build his new church, he was seized with remorse and exclaimed tearfully: 'We wretches, pompously imagining that we do better work, destroy what the saints have wrought.' No such scruples assailed the later restorers of the cathedral, who cheerfully worked their will on the fabric for over a hundred years, beginning in 1748 with Nathaniel Wilkinson, a local Gothic builder of considerable talent, and ending with Sir Gilbert Scott in 1874. The story is one not uncommon in English ecclesiological history, of ill-informed and ingenuous Georgian patching followed by destructive 're-Gothicising' early in the nineteenth century, and by a portentous 'purification' by some eminent church architect of the 1860s or 1870s.

Of the exterior, the central tower is the feature least spoilt by restoration, a

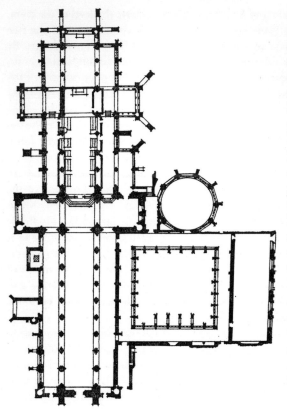

dignified, well-pro-
portioned work of
about 1370, with a
rich, much refaced
early Perpendicular
upper storey. With its
long nave, and two
pairs of transepts, the
building covers a
large area and is built
of a pleasant, brown-
ish stone that to a
certain extent mel-
lows the traces of
recent reconstruc-
tions. Of its façades
the west front is pro-
bably the most suc-
cessful, with a vast
modern window of
Geometrical design,
set between turrets
and catching the
long sunsets over the
Severn.

Inside, the earliest
and one of the most interesting parts of the cathedral is the Norman
crypt (89) beneath the choir. It is apsidal, and thus indicates the ground
plan of the structure originally above it, being divided into a multiplicity
of vaulting compartments by short piers with cushion capitals. It is a most
impressive place and ranks as the best Norman crypt in the country. In
the main church, the earliest piece of design is that of the two Transitional
western bays of the nave; they are extraordinarily interesting work of as
early as c. 1170, with the original, simple quadripartite vault remaining,
on the late twelfth-century shafts, in the south aisle. These two bays have
an attenuated triforium of graded trios of arches which seems to forestall
plate tracery in the disposition of its rosettes of carved ornament. The main
part of the spacious nave consists of seven bays, all of fourteenth-century

work which is reticent in detail though excellent in its proportions; the triforium is clearly modelled on that of the Early English choir. On the north side the bays were built about 1320. Those on the southern side belong to the early Perpendicular period, but with considerable assimilation to the earlier work opposite. It is, however, quite easy to distinguish the two sides from the window tracery in the clerestory, from various sculptural details, and from the obviously richer, more typically Decorated character of the carving on the capitals and elsewhere on the northern side. The two main transepts are part of the Norman fabric, much altered inside by early Perpendicular panelling. The choir (88), with the large chapel of St John off its south aisle, is a characteristic thirteenth-century design whose pillars have clustered Purbeck shafts, well-carved foliate capitals, deep-cut mouldings and (by contrast to the Lady Chapel to the east) a course of dogtooth ornament round most of the arches in the main arcades. The triforium arches have carved figures in their spandrels, and the clerestory consists of trios of lancets parted by slender shafts. The vault is of the plainest sexpartite type, and a superb boss of Christ in Glory is over the original site of the high altar between the eastern transepts. The general effect is, however, much marred by the tasteless and pretentious fittings which must have caused a boom in the mid-Victorian 'art workshops'. The simple thirteenth-century effigy of King John, on its fifteenth-century raised tomb, looks overwhelmed in such surroundings, and the Jacobean Gothic of the pulpit puts the rest of the fittings to shame. The modern stalls incorporate some misericords of about 1380.

The eastern transepts, though only of one bay each, give an effect of space and light accentuated by their elongated lancets. The lower walls display a range of plain thirteenth-century arcading which is carried on continuously round the Lady Chapel and has in its spandrels a series of really superb little carvings of scriptural subjects, including scenes of the Doom. The Lady Chapel is formed by the eastern bays of the structural choir, without any lowering of the roof level. Its arches are narrower and more graceful than those in the choir, and as at Salisbury its earlier date is indicated by a less lavish use of carved detail. The eastern lancets are a nineteenth-century replacement of the large late Gothic window inserted in the 1790s. Facing the south-east transept is the magnificent late Perpendicular screen of Prince Arthur's chantry (6) which commemorates Henry VII's eldest son who died at Ludlow in 1502 and was buried at Worcester. Its stone panelling incorporates Tudor badges along with the devices of Lancaster, York, and of Catherine of Aragon the young prince's widow, while the main vertical shafts, between areas of delicate tracery, are encrusted with enchanting little figures in canopied niches. This is perhaps the finest, and certainly the most historically significant, chantry in England.

Royal memorials apart, this cathedral is peculiarly rich in its monuments and tombs of various dates, Bishop William de Blois (d. 1236) has a splendid effigy of Purbeck marble, and a somewhat similar one of local stone is that of Bishop Walter de Cantilupe (d. 1266), whose nephew was St Thomas of Hereford. Mediaeval knights and ladies are well represented, and several Renaissance monuments of varying designs are to bishops of the seventeenth century; the best of these is the beautiful white marble bust, in its Baroque setting, of Bishop Gauden the Royalist pamphleteer who died in 1662. Many important eighteenth-century artists were responsible for the Georgian monuments, among them Thomas White of Worcester, Adam, Nollekens, Wilton, Moore, and the younger Bacon. But none of their work equals Roubiliac's masterpiece, the Berninesque monument of the venerable Bishop Hough (d. 1743); few more brilliant works of art are to be found in any English cathedral.

Worcester retains a Perpendicular monastic cloister, roofed with a lierne vault which contains some good carved bosses. There are a fine arcaded Norman slype and a well-preserved *lavatorium* only surpassed by that at Gloucester. The interior of the chapter-house, which opens directly off the eastern walk, is a circular Norman structure of polychrome stone, richly arcaded, and revaulted about 1400 from its central Norman pier. At this date the building was reconstructed externally on a polygonal plan, and the large windows were inserted. Above the cloister's south walk rises the late fourteenth-century refectory, which is now used by the Cathedral School. These monastic buildings at Worcester are of great importance in the plot of *The Channings*, a novel by the Worcester-born Mrs Henry Wood who is better known as the authoress of *East Lynne*.

YORK
The Cathedral Church of St Peter

Under the Romans, as *Eboracum*, York grew to be one of the greatest military and economic centres of Britain, and was the temporary base of such Emperors as Hadrian and Septimius Severus when visiting the province to stabilise its northern frontier. It was a substantial Northumbrian settlement at the advent of Christianity, and, in considering the history of its cathedral, one must not forget that the city did not owe its development to the building of a great new church, but had rather to accommodate one within its walls, on a site which grew as the cathedral (a foundation of secular canons) was enlarged throughout the Middle Ages. This explains, even now, the comparatively restricted area of the Close and precincts.

With the consolidation under Edwin of Northumbria's hegemony, York became for a time the chief city of England. It is in this period that its long ecclesiastical history begins. In 601 St Augustine, with papal authority, appointed twelve English bishops, including Paulinus of York who was invested with power to consecrate further bishops as his evangelisation succeeded. Augustine remained primate during his lifetime, but it was laid down that in future the dignity should be awarded between Canterbury and York by priority of consecration, thus sowing the seeds of long and bitter controversy between the two sees. Aeldred, the last Saxon Archbishop of York, officiated at William the Conqueror's coronation, earning for himself the contempt of most of his countrymen. But this timid prevaricator did not long survive the Yorkshire uprising of 1068, when the city was burnt, and the North was 'harried' and largely depopulated by William. A Norman archbishop, Thomas of Bayeux, was appointed in 1070. A new Norman cathedral was started some ten years later, and the piers of its crossing still form the core of the great piers which support the central tower. A nave, with a central section as wide as that of the present nave, but with narrower aisles, was also built, likewise a short, unimpressive choir. A new and more splendid choir was built under Archbishop Roger Pont l'Evêque between 1154 and 1181, but even when completed the church still lacked the splendour of the great Benedictine foundations; its gradual reconstruction, on a scale commensurate with the dignity of an archiepiscopal see, began with the building of the present transepts between 1227 and 1260.

It is difficult to grasp the tremendous scale of the present Minster from any one viewpoint. The tangle of mediaeval streets which surrounds the Close affords glimpses of its three stately towers, but the best distant views are to be had from points along the walls, whence the dominant mass of the church looms majestically above the crowded rooftops. York is one of the largest English cathedrals, and one of the most consistent in that it expresses an almost continuous trend of later mediaeval development. With the exception of some pillars of the Transitional-Norman crypt (most of them reused in the late fourteenth century to support the platform of the high altar), it can show no work earlier than 1227, while the north-western tower was not finished till about 1472. Between those dates the slow pace of building activity was seldom interrupted.

At close range, the cathedral presents some rich and varied façades; easily the most eloquent of these is the fourteenth-century west front(*92*), of an elaboration hardly paralleled in English Gothic. It has been argued that its web of carved detail overloads the structural framework, yet its proportions, combined with the twin fifteenth-century towers, are sure and satisfying. The eastern limb, of which the Lady Chapel was the first part to be started, is mainly Perpendicular but has some Decorated features consistent with its substantial completion late in the fourteenth century. With its skyline of crocketed pinnacles, and with its curious open stonework screens which mask the clerestory windows of its eastern portion, it is on the whole distinctive and effective. The invention of the builders seems, however, to have failed in the eastern wall (except for its vast, magnificently traceried window), where the design, though imposing in its mixture of canopies and pinnacles, is perhaps a little mechanical. The gables of the thirteenth-century transepts form a striking contrast to this later work; the southern one has a great rose window above ranges of characteristic lancets and arcading; on the northern side, adjoining the vestibule to the chapter-house, are the tall, equal-sized lancets of the famous 'Five Sisters'. Above the crossing rises the largest central tower in England. To save weight, its corner pinnacles were never built as contemplated, and as it stands this tower is a triumph of massive simplicity which ranks among the most solid constructional achievements of the fifteenth century.

Within, the remains of the crypt are all that survives of the Norman Minster; they still preserve some distinctive and curious Romanesque capitals and a weird hell-cauldron sculpture. Above ground, the oldest visible work is in the transepts with their eastern and western aisles. They differ from each other in several details, and were conceived on as grand a scale as anything of their period (1227–1260). But their proportions are open to criticism for the heaviness of the triforium which, though interesting and original, is somewhat disconcerting to the scale of the design. Yet the soaring height of the later wooden vault gives an effect of lofty spaciousness rare in English cathedrals.* The views are magnificent, particularly that which

* The transept arcades were considerably altered, at their inner ends, when the nave and choir were rebuilt in the fourteenth century.

2   *York from the south-west. West front 1291–1345, designed by Simon Mason; west window c. 1330–38; central tower 1407–23, by William Colchester; south-west tower 1432–56; north-west tower 1470–74*

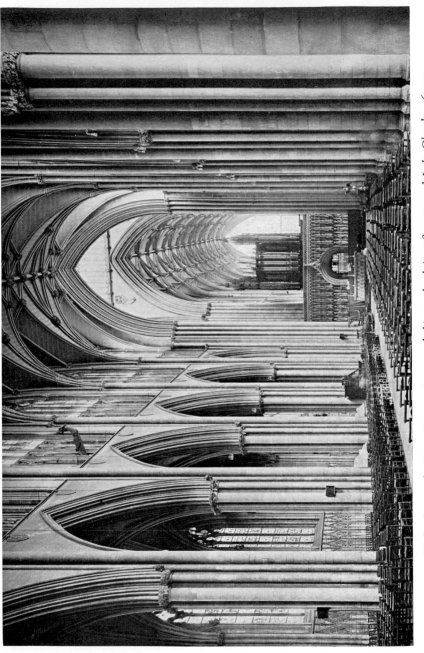

93   York: the nave, by Simon Mason, 1291–1345, looking to the choir, 1380–1400, and Lady Chapel, 361–73

ends northwards in the solemn simplicity of the 'Five Sisters' window (*91*) with its sea-green *grisaille* glass and a panel of twelfth-century glazing from the late Norman choir.

The highest and broadest cathedral nave in England (*93*), while dignified and impressive, is staid in its general effect and lacks supreme distinction. It was begun in 1291 and finished about 1345. It has some effective canopied arcading in the aisles, while the windows have some reserved Geometrical and Decorated tracery which is excellent of its type if inclined to be monotonous; the mullions of the windows in the clerestory continue the vertical lines of the pillarets in the triforium, while below that middle stage the spandrels of the main arcade are decorated with large shields of arms. The great curvilinear west window is particularly magnificent, being only excelled by the somewhat similar east window at Carlisle. This nave, like the choir and transepts, was never completed with a stone vault, and the present wooden one was put up after a fire in 1840. In the eastern limb, the burning of the timber vault in 1829 also destroyed the magnificent choir stalls which appear in Britton's engravings. The interior design, begun at the Lady Chapel end in 1361 and completed early in the next century, is a large-scale but not very distinctive adaptation of that seen in the nave, largely Perpendicular in character but with considerable elements of Decorated in the older, more easterly part beyond the great transeptal windows which were so built to give extra light to the high altar which then stood between them. The east end is almost wholly filled by an enormous rectilinear window which probably contains the greatest single area of fifteenth-century glass in Europe.

The octagonal chapter-house (1290–1310) adjoins the north transept, and by its great height, preponderant areas of glass, and perhaps also by the absence of a central vaulting pier, gives a marked effect of lightness. This absence, however, is a double loss, for the roof is the usual York version in wood. Nevertheless in its detail, its tracery, its beautiful *grisaille* glass, and above all by its abundant naturalistic carving, the York chapter-house ranks high among the achievements of its period, and is not unworthy of the masons' inscription placed with affectionate pride near the door:

> *Ut rosa flos florum*
> *Sic est Domus ista Domorum.*

But the chief glory of York Minster lies in its windows, in which the steady development of English glass painting can be traced through three

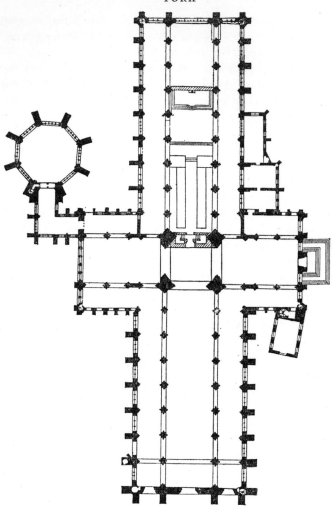

centuries; the great process of replacement and rearrangement after the Second World War was still unfinished in 1959. No other great English church, except King's College Chapel at Cambridge, preserves so high a proportion of its original glazing, or conveys so true an idea of the colour and glow in which the men of the Middle Ages delighted. From the thirteenth century we have the *grisaille* of the 'Five Sisters' with its wreathings of foliage and narrow bands of pale colour; the chapter-house glass, though somewhat later, is also in *grisaille* but enriched with medallions and warmer in tone. There are almost continuous ranges of fourteenth-century 'band' windows in the aisles and clerestory of the nave, among them a delightful 'Bellfounders' window and the heraldic window of Peter de Dene. The splendid fifteenth-century glass of the 'transeptal' windows flanking the sanctuary shows the lives of St William and St Cuthbert, and the deep-toned fourteenth-century work in the west window faces up the full length of the Minster to the many-tinted sea of glass which fills the east end. This great window was finished in 1408 by John Thornton of Coventry and is one of the finest achievements of this craft in Europe, with its 117 Biblical panels, ranging from the Creation to the Apocalypse.

The nave of York Minster has very few monuments of note or beauty, but those in the eastern limb are of great importance, as also is the magnificent stone screen, with its richly canopied niches and original statues of English kings; it dates from late in the fifteenth century and has very fine eighteenth-century iron gates. East of it, many tombs of the mediaeval period commemorate archbishops and other clergy, while an alabaster monument, with its small-sized effigy, is that of the infant Prince William of Hatfield (Yorks) who died in 1344 and was a son of Edward III, whose wedding had been in the Minster. Some Jacobean monuments commemorate local or county worthies, while some late Stuart archbishops are represented by a fine series of reclining effigies in the Baroque taste. By way of contrast, Archbishop Lamplugh (d. 1691) has a standing figure by Gibbons. Among the numerous Georgian monuments, a grouping of great distinction is seen in the memorial to the Hon. Thomas Wentworth (d. 1723); by Lord Burlington's favoured sculptor, the young Bolognese Giovanni Battista Guelfi; it has a sensuous beauty not less worthy of critical appreciation than the very different art of the great mediaeval windows which surround it.

PARISH-CHURCH CATHEDRALS

The churches described in this section were all of them, except for Manchester, raised to cathedral status within the last eighty years, some of them since the 1914–1918 war. In every case they were built principally or wholly for parochial use, and their promotion was in most cases due to the rapid industrial development and increased population of the areas which became new dioceses. Though some of them are fine examples of mediaeval parish-church architecture, they bear little relation to the art and design of the 'greater' cathedrals already mentioned in this book. They tend, however, to illustrate very clearly how our developing notions of what a cathedral should be like have brought about the expansion and elaboration of most of these churches so that they equal, or will in due course equal, the size of such smaller mediaeval cathedrals as Rochester and Carlisle. In most cases the enlargements have been by way of eastward elongation; at Sheffield, however, and in the newly constructed cathedral at Coventry, the new work has involved the complete reorientation of the main structure.

These cathedrals merit inclusion in such a book as this, not only because their cathedral status is unaffected by their size, or by the length of time that they have housed the thrones of bishops, but because they are of very real importance for their architecture and craftsmanship.

BIRMINGHAM   *The Cathedral Church of St Philip*

This fine classical church was designed by the Warwickshire gentleman and 'amateur architect' Thomas Archer, a contemporary of Vanbrugh and a student at first hand of seventeenth-century Roman Baroque which much influenced his work. The building was under construction between 1711 and 1719, but the steeple was not finished before 1725. The tree-studded churchyard is pleasantly characteristic of its period, and is a welcome patch of green amid the gloomy commercial and industrial buildings of the city. The steeple, with its concave sides and only recently (1959) entirely refaced, is characteristic of its time, yet is in some ways distinctive for the Baroque feeling of its design (94); important Baroque touches are also seen in the doorways east of the aisles.

The interior, with its well-defined cornice, and with its tall, free-standing Corinthian columns in the chancel sympathetically added in the 1880s, is spacious and impressive, and the chancel, which contains a good early eighteenth-century organ case, is separated from the nave by delicate ironwork railings, perhaps by the famous Tijou who worked for Wren at St Paul's. Three windows in the chancel, and one at the west end, contain magnificently coloured glass designed by Burne-Jones and executed by William Morris.

BLACKBURN   *The Cathedral Church of St Mary*

The parish church of St Mary, the successor of a mediaeval building, was built between 1820 and 1826 from the designs of a Lancashire architect named John Palmer; the arms of George IV appear on some exterior corbels of the tall pinnacled western tower. The nave of this large clerestoried church, a far from contemptible production of the early Gothic Revival, survives as the nave of a considerably enlarged cathedral, its easternmost bay being canted outwards to join the recent work. The church of the 1820s was built in a slightly free and fanciful version of Perpendicular, and its fine plaster vault, of fourteenth-century type, was put up after a fire in 1831. Some of the west gallery survives, and an older relic is a set of fifteenth-century stalls, with misericords, which probably came from Whalley Abbey.

The first plans, by the late Mr W. A. Forsyth, for the cathedral's extension allowed for a crossing, aisled transepts, and a tall octagonal central tower. Beyond it, a fairly long aisled choir would have had an apsidal sanctuary, a large side chapel, and a polygonal chapterhouse, all in a modern Perpendicular style recalling that of the existing nave. Work started in 1937 and the transepts and crossing arches were built in a somewhat tame twentieth-century Gothic. The tower is still included in the plan, but the work now in progress, with a rather more modern feeling in the uncusped tracery of its windows, has been much modified by considerations of cost. It will give the cathedral a shorter, square-ended sanctuary about half the length originally planned. The completion of this work is expected about 1961.

BRADFORD   *The Cathedral Church of St Peter*

This fine large 'wool church' has a clerestoried nave which dates chiefly from the Perpendicular period, though Early English work of some merit is incorporated in the south arcade. The sturdy, pinnacled western tower is of typically Yorkshire character and was built between 1493 and 1508. The nave roof is a fine piece of fifteenth-century timbering, and the canopied font cover seems to be a work of the Ripon school.

The church has several interesting eighteenth- and early nineteenth-century murals to various local inhabitants of distinction. They include one by Flaxman, and an excellent monument by Scheemakers to Abraham Sharp,

a mathematician and astronomer and a friend of Sir Isaac Newton, who died in 1742. More interesting still is the relief on the tablet to the eminent canal engineer Joseph Priestley (d. 1817). It shows him, in a top hat, superintending navvies at work on a canal tunnel on the Leeds to Liverpool Canal, with barges plying along the waterway.

Important additions are being made to this cathedral, the architect being Sir Edward Maufe; his style, as at Guildford, is a twentieth-century rendering of Gothic. Vestries, and a song school with a beautiful painted ceiling, have been finished on each side of the west tower. Work is now in hand, east of the old nave, on a central tower, sanctuary and Lady Chapel, additional chapels, and a chapter-house. These will add nearly a hundred feet to the length of the cathedral, and their completion is expected in 1963.

BURY ST EDMUNDS *Cathedral Church of St James*

In the West Suffolk county town of Bury St Edmunds the large Perpendicular church of St James, a cathedral since 1914, adjoins the great Norman detached bell tower of the almost wholly vanished abbey. Despite drastic restoration the long nave of nine bays, with two clerestory windows above each arch of the arcades, is a majestic example, started about 1500, of parish-church architecture. On its outside, the ranges of tall aisle windows and the three great windows and canopied niches of the west front are excellent of their type, while some fine Renaissance glass is in one of the western windows.

The present chancel is mid-Victorian work of 1867, but is due to be replaced by a new one forming part of a scheme of eastward enlargement got out by Mr Stephen Dykes Bower. Perpendicular in style, and closely sympathetic to the existing building, the additions to the cathedral will include shallow transepts, a low lantern tower, and a sanctuary of considerable size; the crossing will be parted from the nave by a traceried strainer arch like those at Canterbury. Vestries and a Lady Chapel, cloisters, and a porch and library are also to be built on the northern side. Work on the porch and cloisters was started early in 1959.

CHELMSFORD

The Cathedral Church of St Mary, the Virgin, St Peter and St Cedd

This building is a large and much restored fabric of the type normal in East Anglian parish churches (96). It is for the most part built of flint. The vicissitudes of its history have left it with a nave rebuilt after a collapse in 1800, and with a chancel much refurbished and extended eastwards in memory of the first bishop of the diocese (which was created in 1914); the ceiling over the chancel and sanctuary has recently been magnificently coloured. A chapter-house and some vestries were added on the north side of the chancel in 1929, but nothing has been done to carry out an ambitious scheme, prepared by Sir Charles Nicholson, for the building of a cathedralesque nave and north aisle adjoining the northern side of the present nave. Easily the best features of the present building are the sturdy Perpendicular west tower, with its delightful needle spire of 1749, and the south porch which was added later in the fifteenth century; both are enriched with flint flushwork panelling.

COVENTRY *The Cathedral Church of St Michael*

The city's three great churches, Holy Trinity, St John the Baptist, and St Michael's were all in the front rank of late mediaeval achievement. The last named was chosen in 1918 as the cathedral of a new see, and must not be confused with the mediaeval cathedral priory, the co-cathedral of the pre-Reformation diocese of Coventry and Lichfield, whose monastery was dissolved by Henry VIII and whose buildings have almost wholly disappeared. St Michael's was typical of a large parish church in a rich and important mediaeval city, with an accumulation of side chapels for the many trade and religious guilds. It had preponderant areas of window, and its fifteenth-century chancel ended in a unique five-sided apse, with large transomed windows forming a radiant background to the high altar. The surviving western tower is surmounted by an octagonal lantern, whence a graceful fifteenth-century spire rises to 300 feet, being surpassed only by those at Salisbury and Norwich.

The first aerial attack on Coventry in November, 1940 left no more than the external walls, one vaulted side chapel, and the western steeple of this noble building. Most of the surviving mediaeval work is to be left standing, but Mr Basil Spence's design for its successor allows for a completely new building, to the north of the previous one, whose main axis lies north and south across the site of Coventry's original cathedral. Work is now considerably advanced on this challenging and contemporary structure, with its almost separate Chapel of Unity and with its sides in a zigzag pattern of successive echelons whose tall vertical windows will look back from the high altar and catch the southern light. The slightly sloping roofline of the new cathedral will be relieved, above the sanctuary, by a slender *flèche*, but it seems likely that the interior, with a great tapestry as a backcloth to the free-standing high altar, will artistically be rather more successful than what one will see from outside.

DERBY *The Cathedral Church of All Saints*

The tall western tower of All Saints is a very fine example of late Perpendicular building, dating from 1510–1527 and built by John Otes. The rest of the mediaeval church was demolished in a single night in 1723, after an acrimonious dispute with the Corporation, by order of the incumbent the Rev. Dr Hutchinson, a stalwart classicist who employed James Gibbs to design a new church which would combine nave and chancel under one roof. This

was completed in 1725 under the supervision of Francis Smith of Warwick who acted as building contractor. A simpler and less expensive version of Gibbs' famous design for St Martin-in-the-Fields, its graceful and pleasing interior (95) has no galleries except at the west end, and its pillars have capitals and architrave blocks of the Roman Doric order. There is great cause for thankfulness that much of the Baroque ironwork by the great local

94 Birmingham from the east, showing the recently (1959) refaced steeple. Designed by Thomas Archer, 1711–19; steeple finished 1725; chancel lengthened in nineteenth century

95 Derby: the interior of Gibbs' church, completed in 1725; iron screens by Robert Bakewell

96 Chelmsford from the south, showing the Perpendicular tower with its needle spire of 1749, and the fifteenth-century south porch

97 Truro from the north-east. Designed by J. L. Pearson, and built 1880-1910

98 Manchester from the south-west, showing the Perpendicular nave clerestory and south aisle. The west tower is a modern reconstruction

smith Robert Bakewell remains in the screens, in the altar rails, and on the Mayor's pew. Several monuments of great importance survive from the previous church or have been inserted since the present one was built. A wooden effigy of about 1500 commemorates a canon of the pre-Reformation collegiate establishment, and a Corinthian Jacobean monument is that of the famous 'Bess of Hardwick' (eventually the Dowager Countess of Shrewsbury), who died in 1607 after a notable career of matrimony and building activity. Roubiliac, Nollekens, and Chantrey are among the sculptors of the other memorials, and a fine one by Rysbrack, with a reclining effigy, is that of Caroline, Lady Bessborough who died in 1760.

Before the Derby diocese was formed in 1927 a fairly ambitious scheme for the eastward extension of the church, in a classical style resembling that of Gibbs, was prepared by Sir Ninian Comper. A modified version of this scheme has now been got out by his son, Mr Sebastian Comper, and an appeal has been made for money to carry it out. Like the earlier plans, this design involves the demolition of Gibbs' eastern wall with its doorways and Venetian window.

LEICESTER   *The Cathedral Church of St Martin*

The large, heterogeneous church of St Martin contains work of many periods, and has been very much restored and altered both before and after its elevation to cathedral status in 1926. It largely bears the stamp of the fifteenth century, but the chancel is virtually modern and the outer south aisle of the nave is excellent Geometrical work of about 1300. The central tower and spire, on a Norman base, make up a good essay in the thirteenth-century manner of the East Midlands by the Victorian architect John Raphael Brandon. There is a fine Georgian pulpit, and the numerous monuments to Leicester townsfolk include a richly Baroque one, with three busts in the manner of Rysbrack, to George Newton (d. 1746). A side chapel has several slabs, of Swithland slate and beautifully lettered, to the Herrick family from which the seventeenth-century parson-poet was descended.

MANCHESTER   *The Cathedral Church of St Mary*

St Mary's in pre-Reformation times was both collegiate and parochial, and though its ground plan reflects in the main its parochial character, its internal arrangements belong in part to the former category. It became a cathedral in 1848. The Perpendicular west tower is a modern reconstruction, but the main fabric (*98*), though the parapets and pinnacles were added in recent years, and though much stonework has been renewed, represents a splendid town church of the fifteenth and early sixteenth centuries, with spacious ranges of Perpendicular windows, fine timber roofs over both nave and choir, and an accumulation of lateral chapels which form a second pair of aisles. The church obtained collegiate status in 1421 and was practically rebuilt from that date onwards. The north-eastern chapel, now that of the Manchester Regiment and virtually rebuilt after severe bomb damage, was founded by Sir John Stanley and Bishop Stanley of Ely in 1513; the bishop's brass is a notable feature of its contents. The cathedral's interior effect, with fine panelling and shields in the spandrels of the main arcades, is remarkably airy and graceful, but the chief glory of the church is its array of woodwork fittings, a fine achievement of late mediaeval craftsmanship. The beautiful canopied choir stalls of 1505-1509 are by William Brownfleet of the Ripon school. In addition there is the rich wooden choir screen, now shorn of its rood and celure and with the organ no longer upon it, and a good range of parclose screens in some of the chapels; these last had to be much repaired after bomb damage. The altar rails are very fine ironwork of the early eighteenth century, and the post-Reformation memorials include seventeenth-century brasses to the Mosley and Heyrick families, and a Grecian mural, recalling one by Flaxman at Winchester, to Charles Lawson (d. 1807), High Master of the Grammar School. He is shown with some pupils, a bust of Socrates, and the owl of Athena!

The bomb damage to the cathedral has now been made good, and much fine modern craftsmanship has gone into the work of refurnishing. The new Lady Chapel, by Sir Hubert Worthington, has some interesting tapestries with scenes from the life of the Blessed Virgin Mary rendered in a contemporary idiom.

NEWCASTLE-UPON-TYNE *The Cathedral Church of St Nicholas*

Until it was promoted in 1882 to cathedral status, the parish church of St Nicholas, of a dark stone and blackened with smoke, was among the four largest in England. Its adaptation as a cathedral was done with dignity and success, a choir with throne, stalls, a fine reredos, and other fittings being fitted up in the three western bays of the chancel. A fine Perpendicular east window appears above the reredos, and space is allowed for a Lady Chapel behind it. No enlargements are in hand at the present time.

The church, as a whole, is a dignified cruciform fabric of the fourteenth century. It has no capitals to the arcade columns, an accumulation of chapels, and some pleasing vistas despite the darkness inside. The stately Perpendicular tower, with its rib-vaulted tower space, was added about 1470; its upper adornment is of Scottish type, with a crowning central pinnacle supported on a graceful corona of flying struts. There is a fine tabernacled font cover of the fifteenth century, the brass eagle lectern was made about 1500, and the splendid Renaissance organ case is partly that of 1676.

The memorials in this cathedral include a knight's effigy of about 1300 and many of the thirteenth century and later dates to local citizens. Of the Greek Revival sculptors, Flaxman and Bailey are both represented, and Cockerell's cenotaph to the Northumbrian Admiral Collingwood, Nelson's second in command at Trafalgar who died five years after his chief, has a fine bust and on each side of it a naval trophy.

PORTSMOUTH *The Cathedral Church of St Thomas of Canterbury*

Nautical associations inevitably abound in the pleasant, interesting church of St Thomas of Canterbury. Its architecture falls into three distinct periods. The chancel and transepts are plain early Gothic work of about 1190. The chancel is of exceptional interest with its simply vaulted aisles, modern main vault, and the arcades and containing arches of its two double bays. It has a clerestory but no triforium stage, and its architecture closely resembles that of Boxgrove Priory near Chichester. Between the transepts and what was once the western tower the old nave, with its tall Doric arches and a date of 1693, is a picturesque work in the Wren manner, with a plain panelled pulpit also dated 1693 and a fine pulpit cloth of the following year. Some of the galleries have been cleared away, and the delightful old fittings, largely of ship timber, have inevitably been somewhat 'cathedralised'. The fine Baroque organ case is still, however, in position. The nave and the plain tower represent a reconstruction of 1683–1695 after damage in the Civil War; the tower was built by royal command as a landmark and as a watchtower against enemy ships. Its crowning lantern survives, but the famous 'Golden Barque' weathervane of 1710 is now in the new nave and is used as an almsbox. The tower is now in a central position, and has been ingeniously opened out into the new portions built since the diocese was created in 1927. The modern part of the cathedral was designed by Sir Charles Nicholson and combines debased Gothic elements with a fundamentally Renaissance design echoing that of the late seventeenth-century nave. Transepts and three bays of a new nave have been finished, and part of the new work further east is the 'Navy aisle', with a specially interesting concentration of naval memorials and relics. A very fine Baroque doorway of 1691 has been reinstated on the northern side of the cathedral's new nave. Baroque design is also seen in the numerous fine cartouche memorials, and an earlier tomb, of 1631, is the ornate one to the royal favourite the Duke of Buckingham who was murdered in 1628 in a house not far away.

SHEFFIELD *The Cathedral Church of St Peter*

The present building, whose transepts date from the time of a great Victorian reconstruction, is partly the town's mediaeval parish church and partly represents the rebuilding carried out in 1880. The previous nave, which had been built in 1805 instead of a Perpendicular one, was then replaced by a nave of somewhat greater size. In the eastern part of the church, which became a cathedral in 1914, the tower and spire are dignified work of the fifteenth century, and the chancel and its side chapels are also of the early Perpendicular period. In the southern, or Shrewsbury, chapel are the important monuments of the Fourth Earl of Shrewsbury (d. 1538), and of the Sixth Earl who died in 1590 after being the custodian of Mary, Queen of Scots, and one of the four successive husbands of the famous Bess of Hardwick. The alabaster effigies of the Fourth Earl and of his two Countesses are of magnificent quality, and the Sixth Earl's monument, with a long and historically interesting inscription, is a towering composition in the Elizabethan taste. The fifteenth-century portable wooden sedilia are also a notable feature of this old part of Sheffield Cathedral.

Before the Second World War work was started on great enlargements, to the late Sir Charles Nicholson's designs. These involved the complete realignment of the building, so that the main axis of its new nave and choir would run north and south across the site of the demolished Victorian nave. A second tower was planned so that Sheffield, like Exeter, would have a pair of flanking towers. A start was made on this scheme and the (liturgically) eastern chapel of the Holy Spirit has been finished and contains some fine mediaeval glass transferred from another church in Sheffield.

The foundations actually laid of the Nicholson additions, and some walling and choir arcading already built, are now to be used as part of a new nave and choir which will mainly be the work of Mr George Pace of York. The second tower and spire have been dropped from the scheme, and the body of the church will be of a far more contemporary nature than that originally intended. Concrete construction (stone faced on the outside) will be used to give an unusual window arrangement, and this will make possible a striking arched treatment of the western facade and some unusual arcading, of a cobweblike design, inside the new nave. The completion of the new work is expected in 1964.

WAKEFIELD *The Cathedral Church of All Saints*

The large, plain parish church of All Saints shows an evolution, by successive remodellings, from a simple, unaisled and transeptal Norman fabric with a central tower. This tower collapsed in 1315, the transepts have been absorbed into the widened aisles, and the church in general was largely reconstructed in the fourteenth and fifteenth centuries. The present western tower and spire date from the early years of the fifteenth century. The church became a cathedral in 1888, and by 1905 a new eastern limb, with a sanctuary and a set of chapels containing some fine rib vaulting, had been added in a sympathetic Gothic manner to designs by Pearson. The fine range of seventeenth-century fittings includes a screen of 1635 (with a modern rood by Sir Ninian Comper) and a font cover, while the pulpit is of 1708. The best of the monuments has a reclining figure, before a Baroque background composition, of Sir Lyon Pilkington who died in 1714.

MODERN CATHEDRALS

GUILDFORD   *Cathedral Church of the Holy Spirit*

This wholly new cathedral is situated on high downland, overlooking the pleasant old town whose red-brick Georgian church of the Holy Trinity at first served as the seat of the bishopric. Sir Edward Maufe's design, on the traditional mediaeval ground pattern of a cruciform building, with transepts, central tower, and an eastern Lady Chapel, was started in 1936 and a good deal had been done up to the outbreak of the Second World War. It shows an effective simplification of Gothic forms, and will depend for its completed effect on the balanced grouping of its masses, culminating in the dignified central tower which has yet to be built. The choir and transepts (but not the Lady Chapel) have now been finished, and the nave with its west wall is due to be completed in time for the consecration of the substantially finished building in 1960.

LIVERPOOL   *The Cathedral Church of Christ*

Liverpool cathedral was designed with considerable originality for its period, and on a plan consistent with modern cathedral requirements. Its origins are of much architectural interest, and it was nearly ten years before the design assumed the form in which it is now being brought towards completion. Bodley and Norman Shaw were the selectors of designs in the preliminary assessment of 1901–1902, and, when the plans of the youthful Giles Gilbert Scott were chosen, Bodley was at first associated with him as nominal joint architect. Models and drawings show how the scheme as originally accepted would have been very different to the cathedral actually being built. A pair of tall flanking towers would have recalled those at Exeter, and along the choir and nave a series of shallow transepts would have been similar in conception to those which give extra light to the presbytery at York.

Work actually started in 1904 on the Lady Chapel which was finished in six years; its Gothic has an almost Spanish feeling and is in many ways the most aesthetically satisfying part of the cathedral. The building stands magnificently, overlooking the Mersey and much of the city from its spur of high ground above a disused quarry, which was converted into a cemetery and has some good miniature temples of the Greek Revival. The choir (12) was finished in 1924 and its tall arcades, like the windows and other details, are a very fine statement of Gothic as it could best be interpreted by the first years of this century. The great central tower has a beautiful octagonal top, but the section below it, with the transepts opening out at each end, gives an impression of narrowness and constriction where one normally expects spaciousness in a Gothic cathedral. The glass in this part of the building is lighter and more satisfactory than that in the choir, and the towering canopy above the font is a superb piece of furniture. One bay of the nave, to the (liturgical) west of the western pair of transepts, was structurally complete by the summer of 1959, but some years will elapse before the whole of the architect's design is realised. The cathedral, by then, will have taken about sixty years to build.

TRURO   *The Cathedral Church of St Mary*

Along with Downside Abbey in Somerset the cathedral at Truro is the last great work of imitative Gothic to be built in England. It was started in 1880, and the eastern portion was consecrated seven years later. The western steeples, which were the last part built, were completed in 1910. The architect was J. L. Pearson, and after his death his plans for the work still to be done were closely followed by his son Frank. The design is a distinctive version of the Early English of the thirteenth century, with two pairs of transepts as at Salisbury and Worcester. It is also tinged with French influence which is apparent in the loftiness of its proportions and the attenuation of its towers and spires (97). There is not a feature which has not its precedent somewhere in this country or in Northern France. To the modern eye, this unyielding literalism is the chief defect of the design, for the plan has all the intricacies of its prototypes and accordingly bears little relationship to the requirements of English Protestantism. Rather smaller than the cathedral at Chester, and ranking in the dimensions of its ground plan with that at Rochester, Truro Cathedral has an interior that is simply treated with an admirable mastery of proportion. The incorporation of the ornately finished late Perpendicular south aisle of the previous St Mary's parish church has given a third south aisle to the choir and results in some fine vistas; some Jacobean and later monuments from St Mary's are also preserved in this cathedral of the Cornish diocese. There can be no doubt that Pearson's work is among the most impressive achievements of the later Gothic Revival, but despite its technical cleverness its conception is inevitably anachronistic, and it hardly rises to the dignity of living architecture.

GLOSSARY OF TERMS USED

AMBULATORY–The processional passage around a presbytery formed by the extension of the choir aisles.

APSE–A semicircular or polygonal east end to a church.

ARCADE–A range of arches supported by columns or piers, either open or 'blind', i.e. closed with masonry. Arcading was often used as wall decoration.

BAROQUE–The later expression of the Renaissance style, distinguished by a more profuse degree of ornament and by its bolder, less 'grammatical' treatment of such things as the use of curves, the breaking of pediments, and the grouping of masses. In the English cathedrals it is best seen in numerous monuments, in the architecture of some parts of St Paul's, and in Birmingham Cathedral.

BARREL-VAULT–A covering of either stone or brick, generally of semi-circular section. (Also known as Wagon-Vault.)

BOSS–In ribbed vaulting, a stone, usually carved with foliage or figures, occurring at the intersection of ribs.

BUTTRESS–Masonry built out to strengthen a wall and to resist thrust.

CAPITAL–The crowning member of a column or pier, giving support to superimposed arches or vaulting ribs.

CARREL–A small compartment, similar in principle to a cubicle but smaller, which was built in libraries or cloisters to accommodate the monks' desks when they were writing or illuminating.

CARTOUCHE–A term used, for works in the Baroque and Rococo taste of the seventeenth and eighteenth centuries, to denote the irregularly shaped panels, surrounded by more or less ornate and fanciful decoration, which appear on woodwork, silver, sepulchral monuments, etc.

CELURE–A portion of a church ceiling, over the sanctuary or the rood screen, which was more richly adorned than the rest to do honour to the specially sacred character of the space below it. The colouring was often in blue, with stars—hence the name *Caelura* to suggest the vault of Heaven.

CHANTRY CHAPEL–A chapel within or attached to a church, endowed for the saying of Masses for the soul of the testator or others.

CHAPTER-HOUSE–The council-chamber of a monastic or collegiate establishment, whether or not it was a cathedral.

CHEVET–The grouping at the east end of an apsidal church, containing an ambulatory giving access to a sequence of radiating chapels.

CHOIR–The part of the church between the screen and the presbytery, containing the stalls of the monks or canons. The term is sometimes applied loosely to the entire eastern limb of the church.

CLERESTORY–The side wall of a church above the aisle roof and arcade, pierced with windows and often, in the Perpendicular period, consisting mainly of an expanse of glass and thin dividing mullions.

CORBEL–A block, usually moulded or carved, projecting from a wall and supporting a superincumbent weight.

CORBEL-TABLE–A connected range of corbels immediately beneath the roof of a building; it can also support a parapet.

CRESTING–Continuous ornament, carved or pierced, surmounting a screen, canopy or cornice.

CROCKETS–Decorative features occurring principally at the angles of canopies, pinnacles and spires; usually carved and placed equidistantly.

CURVILINEAR STYLE OR TRACERY–The first phase in the style of the fourteenth century, in which Geometrical forms in tracery were superseded by flowing lines. (Also called Flowing Tracery.)

CUSPS–In tracery, the small inner members that constitute the foliations in the form of trefoils, quatrefoils, etc.

DIAPERING–The more or less complete covering of a stone or brick surface with decorative patterns. In the case of stone surfaces these designs are often in low relief, are arranged in squares or diamonds, and cover the whole area.

DOGTOOTH ORNAMENT–An ornament in the shape of small pyramids often set in a hollow moulding, and repeated either continuously or at short intervals in thirteenth-century work.

FAN-VAULT–The final development in England of Gothic vaulting, in which the curve of all the ribs is similar. The actual ribs are generally decorative rather than structural, and the fan-like shapes, or conoids, are always apparent. Sometimes pendants are introduced.

FERETORY–The part containing the relics in a shrine or monument.

FLYING-BUTTRESS–A buttress in the form of an open arch directing the thrust of a high vault across the roof of an aisle to the main buttress.

GEOMETRICAL STYLE OR TRACERY–The phase after Early English, or Lancet, at the close of the thirteenth century, characterised by an early type of bar tracery designed strictly in geometric forms, in which circles and triangles predominate.

GRISAILLE–Thirteenth- or early fourteenth-century glass whose main design is based on lightly engraved compartments of grey or greenish-grey hue.

GROINED VAULT–A vault resulting from the intersection of two or more surfaces at an angle, the 'ribs', or lines of intersection, being the groins.

HAMMERBEAM ROOF–A wooden roof in which the tie-beam is dispensed with, and its place taken by projecting beams. The ends of these are generally treated decoratively.

LABEL STOP–The moulded or sculptured termination of a hood-mould (interior) or drip-mould (exterior) which runs over the top of an arch or window. Label stops are often rendered as foliage, human heads, or grotesques.

LANCET WINDOW–A name applied to the narrow pointed window of Early English Gothic from its resemblance to a lancet blade.

LIERNE RIBS–Small connecting ribs used in vaulting, particularly during the fourteenth century, for decorative effect only.

MISERICORD–The lifting seat of a choir stall, usually with a carved bracket on the underside. (Also known as *Miserere*.)

MOULDINGS–The varieties of contour given to angles, arches and other projecting members of various parts of buildings to produce contrasts of light and shade and richness of effect.

MULLIONS–The vertical divisions between lights in a Gothic window, from which the tracery springs.

NAVE–The western limb of a church, in some cathedrals and abbeys partly used by the lay congregation.

NORMAN ARCHITECTURE–The English variant of Romanesque in the eleventh and twelfth centuries, immediately preceding Gothic.

OGEE–A curve of double flexure, produced by a convex and concave curve flowing the one into the other.

PARCLOSE–A screen separating a chapel or aisle from the body of the church.

PENDENTIVE–A triangular panel of masonry, on a concave plan, which transmits the weight of a dome on to its supporting piers.

PERPENDICULAR–The last of the great periods of English Gothic architecture. It flourished during the later fourteenth, the fifteenth and the sixteenth centuries.

PIER–A supporting member from which arches or vaulting spring, in form usually cylindrical, octagonal, rectangular or clustered, i.e. composed of a collection of shafts.

PINNACLE–A tapering terminating member, vertical, and usually crowned by a finial, and smaller than a turret.

PISCINA–A recess including a shallow stone basin, with a drain, set in a niche south of an altar for washing sacred vessels.

POUPÉE-HEAD–The carved termination of a choir-stall or other bench-end. (Sometimes called a Poppy-head.)

PRESBYTERY–The eastern portion of a church beyond the choir, containing the high altar.

PULPITUM–The gallery above the solid screen separating the nave from the ritual choir in a cathedral or monastic church. The term is often applied to the screen itself.

QUADRIPARTITE–A simple form of ribbed vaulting, consisting of transverse, diagonal and wall ribs, dividing a rectangular vault space, or compartment, into four segments.

RENAISSANCE–The great art movement by which the classical styles of architecture, as transmitted from Greece by the designers of the Roman Empire, was reintroduced into England from the sixteenth century onwards; the process was accentuated in the following century by Inigo Jones and Wren. The style appears in numerous church monuments, was used by Jones for his new portico at Old St Paul's, and appeared again in St Paul's as rebuilt by Wren. One sees it also, in Gibbs' version of the style, in Derby Cathedral.

RETROCHOIR–The portion of the eastern limb behind the high altar to the east.

RIB–A structural member dividing up the compartment of a vault, generally moulded.

ROMANESQUE–The style of architecture prevalent in Western Europe from about the ninth to the twelfth century, perpetuating the round arch of the Romans.

SEDILIA–Recessed seats for priests on the south side of the high altar, generally of masonry and canopied.

SEXPARTITE–A form of ribbed vaulting, similar to the quadripartite, but having an extra transverse rib which divides the rectangular compartment into six segments.

SHAFT–A smaller column, either independent or a member of a pier.

SLYPE–A passage from the cloister, through a range of monastic buildings, leading out to other buildings outside the main claustral group.

SPANDREL–The triangular space formed between two arches, or between one arch and the rectangular lines of a hood-mould.

STRING-COURSE–A projecting horizontal band or moulding on a wall, often continued around a building.

TABERNACLE-WORK–The carved and ornamental canopy-work over stalls, fonts, niches, etc.

TRACERY–The ornamental stonework in the heads of Gothic windows, springing from and supported by the mullions. Circular windows were also filled with tracery. The earliest form is Plate Tracery, consisting of circles and other geometrical figures cut in solid stonework. After the middle of the thirteenth century, the tracery was built up of stone bars (Bar Tracery).

TRANSEPTS–The cross-arms of a church, projecting transversely to the nave, presbytery and aisles.

TRANSOMS–The horizontal bars in windows.

TRIFORIUM–The storey above the arcade, enclosed by the roof of a side aisle. In cathedrals, it is often a gallery between the arcade and the clerestory.

TYMPANUM–The space enclosed between the lintel and the arch of a doorway in Norman and Gothic buildings, often filled with sculpture.

UNDERCROFT–A comparatively low, vaulted space running beneath some building, e.g. part of a church or the domestic range of a monastery. Structurally it is on the same principles as a crypt, but its floor need not be lower than ground level.

VAULT–Any form of arched roofing over a building with the exception of the domical. Vaults are either groined, as in Romanesque architecture, or ribbed, as in all Gothic architecture.

INDEX

The numerals in **heavy type** refer to the *Figure Numbers* of the illustrations